CONTENTS

CONTENTS

REPORT FROM THE FRONT LINE: FORT WAYNE'S BATTLE AGAINST DRUGS

MONDAY, JUNE 24, 1996

HOUSE OF REPRESENTATIVES,
SUBCOMMITTEE ON NATIONAL SECURITY, INTERNATIONAL AFFAIRS, AND CRIMINAL JUSTICE,
COMMITTEE ON GOVERNMENT REFORM AND OVERSIGHT,
Fort Wayne, IN.

The subcommittee met, pursuant to notice, at 3:30 p.m., in the Fort Wayne Room, Fort Wayne Chamber of Commerce Building, 826 Ewing Street, Fort Wayne, IN, Hon. Mark E. Souder (member of the subcommittee) presiding.

Present: Representative Souder.

Also present: Representative Hastert.

Staff present: Robert B. Charles, staff director and chief counsel; Sean Littlefield, professional staff member; Ianthe Saylor, clerk; and Cherri Branson, minority professional staff member.

Mr. SOUDER. Good afternoon. I'd like to call this meeting to order. Today, we're holding a hearing here in Fort Wayne. It's part of a series. We started a number of field hearings to get community input last fall in New England. This morning we were in the Chicago land area, here in Fort Wayne this afternoon. We hope to do one in western United States later on this year. We also have had hearings started just about a month after I got on this subcommittee, we started with our first hearing with Nancy Reagan trying to call attention again to what we felt was a slippage in the battle against drugs in this country, moved through hearings with the Coast Guard, with the then-drug czar, Lee Brown. We did a number of field hearings on interdiction in Puerto Rico, along the border with Mexico.

Then last spring, as many of you know, we went to Central and South America. Congressman Hastert from Illinois, who is here today, Chief Deputy Whip, arguably at least one of the top four, if not one of the top three or so influential and powerful Republicans in our Congress, led that codel. It was called the Hastert Congressional Delegation. We met with the Presidents of Mexico and Peru and in Colombia, Bolivia and Panama. That was very enlightening to us to see the impact on Fort Wayne and the area around here of the failure of backing off our international interdiction effort.

Our topic today, as most of you know, is to report from the front lines focussing on Fort Wayne's battle against drugs and the link to international trafficking. This subcommittee, in particular, has jurisdiction over the State Department, the Defense Department, CIA and most of the things that are run in the State Department and Defense Department efforts on drug interdiction. We also have jurisdiction over the Justice Department, which includes most of the Federal efforts in drug interdiction. And because we have the drug czar's office, we have some jurisdiction into the treatment and education. That is not predominately the focus of this subcommittee.

I'm also on the subcommittee that has oversight of education and health and this subcommittee, and Congressman Hastert is also on a full committee that has oversight, but we're focusing more on interdiction today. A lot of people asked me why we were doing that. That's because it's the primary jurisdiction to the subcommittee, although we'll also be including some prevention and treatment programs.

Our central aim is threefold. We're going to explore the national security threat posed by the international narcotics trafficking. Second, we'll hear testimony on how the threat is materializing here in the Fort Wayne area. And third, we'll examine local efforts to combat this. I would like to personally welcome all of our witnesses.

We're here to learn and to take back to Washington what we learn here today. In addition to the testimony that we're receiving from of all our panelists, we are going to be receiving a number of written statements that we're going to insert. It's been since 1989, October 11th, when I worked for Senator Coats, that we had a hearing here on crack prices in Fort Wayne. I believe Chief Moore was the only same witness that we have today, exact witness.

To some degree, some of this will be an update of what we had in 1989, because in Fort Wayne we've been battling this for a long time. We're also going to—before we start with the panel, I'm going to refer to Paine Brown for a welcome from the mayor. But I would be remiss in not acknowledging his efforts directly as mayor of Fort Wayne in what's been an extended and protracted battle to fight the drugs that are pouring into the city of Fort Wayne, in particular, and now spreading through northeast Indiana.

There are many others and some things that we don't have on the panel today that I want to acknowledge. We have had, in my opinion, a very strong and successful drug task force in this region. It's not been without controversy. I know our local sheriff has also been addressing that in his efforts, while there are disagreements sometimes on how best executed, it's good to see the strong focus we have regardless of arguments and differences on exact procedures.

I think that all are to be committed to this battle. I know Tom Ostrogni is here today who has worked with trying to crack down on the drug houses and the Drug Den Ordinance in Fort Wayne. I visited the treatment program out at Byron Health Center, which is targeted more toward female abusers, which we do not have highlighted here today. Just because somebody is not at this hearing does not mean that they are not having an important impact in the city of Fort Wayne or northeast Indiana.

I saw Sheriff Muncie from Wells County here today. I know Sheriff Butes from Noble County has been in touch with us. We all are working together to realize that if we don't hang together in northeast Indiana, we're not going to be successful.

I want to make a few comments. I'm going to insert all of this into the record but I want to lead off and I know our DEA representatives will highlight this a little bit more. So often in Fort Wayne, we do not necessarily understand how it interconnects with the international battle. You can argue who should take care of the local streets and you can argue who should take care of your State, but it's clear that in Bluffton and in Kendallville and in Fort Wayne, there's no way we can interdict the stuff from Colombia.

That's clearly the role of the Federal Government. Last year, for the third year in a row, approximately 400 tons of cocaine entered the United States. Roughly 70 percent of that came in from Mexico and 26 percent from Puerto Rico. Most of that, we, Congressman Hastert and I, saw in Bolivia and in Peru, in the coca fields. We watched the DEA blow up a small lab there, which are back in the middle of the jungles and it's very difficult.

We have had some success and were having great success up until 1992. Basically what we treat it as is, "Oh, well, we won the drug war. We threw a lot of money." We started to back off, and then we see the startling statistics that Bill Bailey at Indiana University, again, released today about rising abuse in marijuana, tobacco and alcohol in our State, higher than the national average.

The national average has also been soaring. It's not surprising that the amount of cocaine is up, the purity is up and the prices are down. We're having to battle that at the local and grassroots level. So I think our message is relatively simple. We're here and we strongly believe we need to girt up our resources. We need to be prepared to battle. We are not going to solve this, there is no silver bullet, as Mr. Chretien is fond of saying. All of us believe that the problem is 10 years, 12 years, but it's not impossible.

At this point, what I would like to do is first introduce Paine Brown, who's the public—he's over the police and fire department. I wanted to call him public affairs, but he's not public affairs. He is a school board member in Fort Wayne, and public safety director, so he's doing both, to welcome us on behalf of the mayor.

[The prepared statement of Hon. Mark E. Souder follows:]

Good Morning everyone and thank you all for coming. Today, we are holding one in a series of field hearings on national drug policy or counter-narcotics policy, and how that policy affects us locally.

This morning, we will hear testimony from the people who are on the front lines every day -- including the DEA's top international official, who travelled with us to South America and is a real leader in this effort.

Our topic today, as most of you know, is "A Report from the Front Lines," focusing on Fort Wayne's battle against drugs and the link between that battle and international drug trafficking.

Our central aim is three-fold: First, we are going to explore the national security threat posed by international narcotics trafficking; second, we will hear testimony on how that threat is materializing here in the Fort Wayne area; third, we will examine local prevention and treatment efforts.

Let me welcome all of our witnesses. It is a privilege to have you here, and a privilege to be chairing this hearing. I think we will learn a lot as these proceedings unfold. I can also assure you that Congressman Hastert and I will bring the knowledge we gain back to Washington, and use it in setting the course for national drug policy.

In my opinion, this location is the perfect place for one in a series of field hearings on national drug policy. We have people working very hard to turn back the tide of illegal drugs, and we have indications in this region of both the strengths and vulnerabilities of our current national drug policy.

Believe it or not, the deadly drugs produced in Peru and Bolivia, processed in Colombia, and transshipped up through Mexico and Puerto Rico, are also here with a vengeance.

Last year, for the third year in a row, approximately 400 tons of cocaine entered the U.S. Of that total, roughly 70 percent came over our border with Mexico, and the DEA estimates that 26 percent was trafficked through Puerto Rico.

What many people don't realize is the close link between these seemingly far away places and our own homes and schools. Virtually all the world's coca -- the plant from which cocaine is made -- grows in Peru and Bolivia. Almost all of the coca is processed into cocaine HCL in Colombia, from which it comes to the U.S. through Mexico or Puerto Rico.

While stopping cocaine and heroin production in Peru, Bolivia and Colombia is critical, Mexico is a threat for other reasons. Last year, Mexico produced 150 tons of meth-amphetamine. This is a deadly drug that is making its way West from California, commonly goes by the name speed or poor-man's crack, and is killing kids and putting them in hospital emergency rooms, along with LSD, heroin and crack.

Mexican drug cartels are now shipping two deadly types of heroin into the U.S., so-called "white" and "black tar" heroin. And marijuana coming from Mexico and Colombia is now up to 25 times more potent than what was on U.S. streets in the late 1960s.

I personally believe that we, as a Nation, have to begin recognizing the enormity of the problem that is confronting us -- and that our children and grandchildren must now deal with daily.

The threat of illicit drugs and drug-related crime in America is not receding. In fact, over the past three years, it has deepened. Among children aged 8 to 17, drug use has increased 200 percent. At the same time, the price of dangerous drugs has fallen dramatically, availability has risen and street purities for cocaine, heroin and marijuana have each gone through the roof.

The message I hope we all begin to think more about is fairly simple: America is under siege. To beat this threat, we have to put our differences aside and work together to implement a balanced strategy of prevention, including interdiction, and treatment. History shows us that we can generate excellent results with the right priorities.

Former DEA Administrator and Federal Judge Robert Bonner recently testified that between 1985 and 1992, regular drug users fell by 80 percent, from 5.8 million to 1.3 million. Crack use declined from nearly a million in 1990 to just over 300,000 in 1992 and marijuana use plummeted from 22 million regular users in 1985 to 8.5 million in 1992, a 61 percent fall.

Today, drug use is up for juveniles in every drug category -- heroin, crack, cocaine, LSD, non-LSD hallucinogens, stimulants, inhalants and marijuana. Today, one in three high school seniors has smoked marijuana, which is up to 25 times more potent than in the 1960s. In 1994, there were three-quarters of a million more teenagers using drugs than in 1992, a reversal of the 1981 to 1992 downward trend.

Let me close by saying that a lack of funding is a big part of the problem. In 1992, President Bush committed 1.5 billion dollars to drug interdiction. In 1993, President Clinton cut $200 million out of the interdiction effort. Unfortunately, the President mothballed Customs and other aircraft, removed certain intelligence assets and reduced the number of cutters, ship days, flying hours and personnel. This subcommittee detailed much of those losses in our annual report.

In 1994, the Administration cut interdiction again by another $18 million, and in 1995, by another $15 million. In the 1996 strategy, released last month, President Clinton has put drug interdiction down at a level still nearly $100 million below the 1992 level, and source country programs are $123 million below 1992 levels.

I believe we have to stand up and say it like it is. This is a war, and it is deadly. It is also winnable. I think that the dedication shown already by those who are our witnesses today deserves enormous recognition. We are lucky to have such dedicated people working on this resurgent threat.

I am also lucky to have recently travelled with some of those most openly committed to winning, both here at home and in the source countries of Mexico, Peru, Bolivia, and Colombia.

Let me then welcome all of you, and turn to Congressman Hastert for his opening. After that, we will introduce our witnesses, and open our first panel. We will then go to questions, and thereafter turn to our distinguished second panel.

Mr. BROWN. Congressman Hastert and Congressman Souder, first of all, let me tell you that it is indeed a pleasure and an honor to be here this morning on behalf—this afternoon on behalf of Mayor Paul Helmke to welcome you both here and let you know how much it means to us, frankly, that you two are willing to hear the concerns of local law enforcement. I'm sure that this will be enlightening, you will hear some enlightening testimony and I think the message that is going to come across to you loud and clear is that while we in local law enforcement can do so much to deal with street level dealers and so forth, it is certainly going to take a cooperative effort, and coordinated and conservative effort between agencies at all levels of Government to effectively deal with this problem.

Again, we're just appreciative that you two here recognize our endeavor to address some of the issues that will be presented by our local officials. So with that, again, welcome on behalf of the mayor. Thank you.

Mr. SOUDER. Thank you for your leadership. I'll yield to Congressman Hastert for any opening statement.

Mr. HASTERT. Well, thank you, Congressman Souder. I'll be very, very brief. As Congressman Souder said, there's 400 tons of cocaine coming into this country every year across the borders, southwest and through the Caribbean, mostly through Puerto Rico and the Virgin Islands. A kilo of cocaine in Bolivia or Peru probably sells for about $200. A kilo of cocaine that has made its way across the border into the United States, either in the bottom of a truck or cargo container or by mule, which is a person who carries it for money, would probably run maybe $2,000, $3,000 on the street. That's broken down.

It could be—I'm sorry. It's not $2,000 or $3,000, it's $20,000 or $30,000. On the street when it's broken down, it would be $300,000. So when that narcotic, when that drug reaches this country, the dynamic of expense to track it down, the profit that people can derive from it, the problematic situation of catching people, prosecuting people, working it up to the top to the people who are really responsible, it's really very, very difficult.

One of these tactics, not the only, but one of the tactics and one of the ways that we can best serve this country is to keep drugs out of this country. Intercept it at the country of origin, the source countries. Stop it before it gets to our borders. To stop it and to not allow these people very sophisticated procedures and technologies and huge amounts of cash to corrupt our officials, to corrupt our kids and certainly make addicts out of our children.

There's a 200 percent increase in drug use among youth since 1992. Specifically youth that we call between 8 and 17 years of age. We have a cost in this country, or we have approximately, so you can quantify it, about $425 billion in violent crimes that are enacted in this country. Clearly 60 to 70 percent of those violent crimes are driven by people who are addicted to drugs or in pursuit of money for drugs.

Where do these drugs come from? Well, your cocaine will come from Peru, about 70 percent of it. Bolivia about another 30, not quite 25 percent maybe. Some of it comes from Colombia, a very small amount. It's all sent to Colombia, it's manufactured there into cocaine and into crack. And also heroin comes from Colombia, with the purest strain of poppy that anybody's been able to grow in many, many years. Some of it comes from Mexico. Some of it comes from the Far East. Almost a third of it that crosses our border today comes from Colombia and Mexico.

Methamphetamine comes from Mexico. Marijuana comes from Mexico and California and Indiana and other places. So the war on drugs in this country, much of it comes across the border, some of it's here, but we need a total effort, an international effort, national effort and certainly State and local efforts. It's a war that a lot of people would like to wave the white flag at and forget that it ever existed. It's a war that some would like to, again, retreat from. They'd like to legalize marijuana and other drugs so that war wouldn't be there. But it's a war that's devastating to our children. It's a war that's devastating to our society and at great, great cost. It's a war that we can't afford to lose, a war that we actually have to make a complete effort to win.

So, I appreciate having this meeting here today with Congressman Souder. I appreciate those people who come forward to testify, and I look forward to hearing you.

Mr. SOUDER. Once again, I want to thank you for coming to Fort Wayne. He's a busy man. He's the chief head-counter to keep track of what bills are. He's also been in charge of pulling the Health Bill together between the House and the Senate, coordinating all the efforts to passing a health policy in the country in addition to the drug legislation. So it's a big honor to have him here in Fort Wayne today.

Our witnesses on the first panel are Craig Chretien, who's currently DEA's Chief of Operations, oversees all the international operations for DEA. He's the person who has let all the drugs come in. Is that the correct way to say it? No. He's trying to coordinate the efforts to intercept as much as possible. He recently accompanied Congressman Hastert and I, as well as Congressmen Zeliff and Mica, into Central and South America.

I had the privilege of sharing a seat right across from him on most of the flights to the different countries and got to pick his brain for hours and hours through 8 days, and it was a tremendously enlightening experience for me. I'm very pleased that the DEA Director Constantine has seen fit to have him come into our fair city today and appreciate his being here.

Also, John Morgan, who is the Chief of the Chicago, midwestern office, oversees the Indianapolis office, which northern Indiana is a subdivision of Indianapolis. He's over the Chicago office, which includes all the midwestern States. He was also at this morning's hearing, and we appreciate your coming down and we're looking forward to the DEA satellite office in Fort Wayne that we've been working together to try to bring in.

We're pleased to have Lieutenant Heck, Jeff Heck, who serves as commander of the Indiana State Police Department's Major Drug Section. He's also a member of the Indiana Drug Enforcement Administration, the National Drug Enforcement Officers Association and the White Collar Crime Investigator Association. We're pleased to have him here today representing the State of Indiana and giving us a little bit of an overview of the State.

Robert Gevers serves as our Allen County prosecuting attorney, based here in Fort Wayne. He's previously served as chief counsel within the prosecuting attorney's office, after having held several other positions, both in private law firms as well as the U.S. attorney's office in Indiana's Northern District. So because of his experience not only in Allen County, but with the U.S. attorney's office, he can give us some overview not only of Allen County, but how it relates to other counties in northeast Indiana.

Chief Neil Moore heads the Fort Wayne Police Department. He also lends his time and experience to Fort Wayne's battle against drugs as current chairman of D.A.R.E.'s Indiana Executive Board. He's been a pillar in this community, has been through the many variations of this battle, the ups and downs—we win some, we lose some—but he's never given up the fight.

And I've already introduced Paine Brown, who's over all the public safety offices. What I need to do next in this hearing because of the areas we work with and it's an oversight committee, I need you all to stand and to swear you in.

[Witnesses Sworn]

Mr. SOUDER. Let the record show that the witnesses responded in the affirmative. We'll start with Mr. Chretien.

STATEMENTS OF CRAIG CHRETIEN, CHIEF OF INTERNATIONAL OPERATIONS, DRUG ENFORCEMENT ADMINISTRATION; JAMES MORGAN, SPECIAL AGENT, DRUG ENFORCEMENT ADMINISTRATION, CHICAGO; JEFF HECK, LIEUTENANT, INDIANA STATE POLICE DEPARTMENT; ROBERT GEVERS, PROSECUTING ATTORNEY, ALLEN COUNTY; AND T. NEIL MOORE, CHIEF, FORT WAYNE POLICE DEPARTMENT

Mr. CHRETIEN. Good afternoon, Chairman Hastert and Congressman Souder. I appreciate this opportunity to be able to discuss narcotics issues before this panel. On behalf of DEA Administrator Constantine, I want to express our appreciation for the support this committee has been providing the DEA for all these years.

With your permission, I'd like to submit for the record written testimony from the board and myself. I mentioned earlier about the trip that we took to South America and Central America. I'm embarrassed to say that for someone who has been ranger-trained, eaten monkeys in Brazil, and bugs—I don't know where their origin was from—and different parts of the Amazon, I, during one part of the trip, got sick on a piece of shrimp at the Ambassador's residence in Panama. So that knocked me out for one portion of the trip, but I was there in spirit.

The trip, to me, showed the importance that the committee placed upon what this country is trying to accomplish overseas. I think it's become lost sometimes, both for those in Washington and the American public, as to the role that our Government plays and the difficulties we have in trying to accomplish the mission.

What I'd like to do, briefly, is go over a couple of points and discuss the source countries where the cocaine originates, how it's processed, how it's smuggled into the United States, what that entails and then go into the role of Mexico and how that directly impacts drugs coming into our country. And then my colleague, Mr.

Morgan, will go into more specifics as to how those drugs get into the State of Indiana and the surrounding areas.

When you look historically at the role of organized crime and the threat of organized crime in the past, I don't think there's any other group outside of our declared enemies during the various wars that has exerted the type of influence, the corruptive influence, and has directed violence in our streets in the United States as what you're seeing with the Colombian drug traffickers, particularly the Cali Cartel.

Traffickers don't have a textbook of laws to follow. They ignore borders. They ignore boundaries. They operate out of convenience and they operate where their money has influence; influence and corruption buy things necessary to get their job done. Their operation is really a continuum from source countries into the United States with seamless borders. And those are just the facts. Those are some of the obstacles that we have to overcome along with working with the various law enforcement agencies.

I have a couple of overheads. Perhaps we could put up the first one. They should depict the roaming source countries for the coca leaves. They are primarily Bolivia, Peru and to a lesser degree Colombia. Like Congressman Hastert said, Peru is by far the largest producer of the coca leaf, and Bolivia second. And the process isn't that complicated. When you hear the word laboratory, you think glassware and people wearing white coats, very sanitary conditions, when in fact it's some of the dirtiest processing conditions you'll ever see.

They literally dig a hole in the ground, put some plastic underneath it, throw in some leaves that are picked from the coca farmers and you throw in kerosene and some other chemicals and then you get this dirty paste from this process. That's a little further defined. And then from there, that product, cocaine base, is sold to Colombia traffickers, who then further process it to cocaine hydrochloride. Cocaine hydrochloride is then ready to be used for consumption.

Also, from cocaine hydrochloride you can produce crack, which is a very small, simple process to convert it back to its base form, which is all that it is, and that's ready for smoking.

I think there's another slide that depicts how the drugs are then moved from South America into the United States, through Mexico, Central America. What's not shown on there with the arrows, but it's clearly there, is the Caribbean. We were successful a few years ago in stopping pretty much the activity of the flow of cocaine and marijuana from South America going through the Caribbean into the United States, so much so that the traffickers found it more convenient to go through Mexico.

You'll see by these arrows that Mexico figures very prominently in the drug trade. In fact, we now calculate that approximately, or up to, 70 percent of the cocaine that enters into the United States comes through Mexico. There's an interesting historical explanation for that. Mexican trafficking groups have, for years, have been transporting homegrown marijuana, their own variety, and also black tar heroin. Through the years they have developed into four major, significant cartels or families, if you will. You see that each family controls a particular area of Mexico and they decide what drugs go into the United States.

In fact, they control pretty much most of the drugs that go into the United States themselves. Some of the groups are very violent. They're very ruthless. They take whatever means necessary to ensure their drugs get across. Historically, since they had the infrastructure and they had the experience of moving Mexican brown heroin and marijuana into the United States, the Colombians came to them and said, "Look. We would like to move a ton of cocaine from Colombia into a warehouse in, let's say, Los Angeles or San Diego. We will pay you a couple of thousand dollars a kilo to get it there." So that arrangement was very beneficial for both sides. And then the Mexican trafficking groups, at some point, said, "Rather than pay us money, why don't you pay us in kind. For every 500 or thousand kilos that you want us to transport for you, why don't you give us the same amount?" The significance of that is that they now have established their own market for cocaine.

The money that they make—the profits are staggering. That money then goes back into Mexico. It pays for more corruption. It distorts the banking industry. It puts the legitimate businessmen at a disadvantage.

By the way, this pattern is the exact same pattern as what happened in Colombia. If you listen to some of the presidents and leaders of countries, as we did on our trip, which you mentioned, virtually all of them expressed a fear about becoming like Colombia. So, it's something that really is important to us, especially with Mexico because it's right on the border.

If that weren't bad enough, Mexico is now the leading producer of methamphetamine. Methamphetamine, or speed, or crank, as it's been referred to, years ago was pretty much produced by small laboratories in the United States, mostly on the West Coast. We were successful in controlling the precursors coming in, all of the chemicals necessary to make that. The market pretty much dried up in the United States for setting up these labs.

Well, Mexican traffickers took over. They are now the world's largest producers of methamphetamine in ton quantities. In fact, in Los Angeles, where cocaine was the drug of choice, we're now seeing that they're being replaced by methamphetamine. I understand there are parts of Indiana that are now seeing the same sort of problem.

The emergency reporting statistics, which usually track emergency room injuries for people who have overdoses of certain drugs, it's literally going off the screen for methamphetamine. It's a very serious problem. It's cheaper than cocaine. It's sometimes called the "Poor man's cocaine." It has a longer-lasting effect and it's, if it can be, more harmful to the body than cocaine.

Oftentimes, I speak to groups and I have a difficult time trying to explain what occurs overseas and how does it have direct correlation to what happens in Fort Wayne, IN. The Cali Cartel, up until recently, was the most significant trafficking organization in the world. Their net profit is probably approaching, if not exceeding, that of General Motors. They exercise control down to the minute detail in the United States, ensuring that cocaine came in, that they received the money, and that the money was sent back to Colombia or wherever they designated.

We were very successful in working with the Colombian police and it wasn't just DEA. A variety of Government agencies, were a large part of it, but it was combined effort, and it took years to do. We were successful in arresting and incarcerating all of the major cartel members except for one, and I suspect he will be arrested here within the next couple of months by what I'm led to believe. They're still operating, but with much less efficiency.

What's happening is there are new groups now trying to fill that void. During this time period, while this destruction is taking place, Mexican trafficking groups are now going direct to the source countries such as Peru and Bolivia, trying to bypass the Colombians to start their own connections. It will be interesting to see if the Colombian traffickers allow this to happen. Only time will tell. But there's too much money involved for the Colombians just to turn by and let this bypass.

Hopefully, we'll see the violence that surely will be associated with this take place in Mexico and other places, not the United States. Sometimes it's very frustrating to come up with, well, what is the answer? With all these problems, we know we have a drug problem, nothing seems to work and I think that we need to be more realistic with a lot of people. We need to be very circumspect in admitting that law enforcement alone is not the answer. If you would have asked me 15, 20 years ago, I would have probably said that another thousand agents and some more cars, more 'copters, will solve the problem.

It's not that simple any more. We need an effective, coordinated, ballanced approach with strong law enforcement. We need treatment. All of these things combine into one coherent strategy. It's certainly working the source of the transit countries, particularly source countries that support guns. The number of dollars that we spend in a place like Peru or Bolivia goes a lot further than trying to catch that same amount of cocaine that's already made it into the United States.

It just makes more sense to try to get closest to the problem, where it originates. There is no silver bullet, as I'm fond of saying. It is a solvable problem, but it's something that's going to take time. I think that the public is frustrated by hearing we're turning the corner, it's 3 years, 4 years away. We need to say, "it's going to be a long-term approach, 10 years is not unrealistic." By the way, as long as there is the demand, as long as people want to use it, there will be supply.

If tomatoes were illegal, and people wanted to eat tomatoes, somebody would grow them in Peru or Bolivia. It's as simple as that. I want to thank the committee for allowing me to have this opportunity to speak.

[The prepared statement of Mr. Chretien follows:]

Testimony before the House Committee
on Government Reform and Oversight
Craig Chretien, Chief Foreign Operations
James Morgan, Special Agent in Charge
Chicago Field Division
Drug Enforcement Administration
Ft. Wayne, Indiana
June 24, 1996

Introduction

Mr. Souder, we appreciate this opportunity to appear before you today to discuss narcotics control efforts in the Western Hemisphere. The Drug Enforcement Administration is appreciative of the support that the Committee on Government Reform and Oversight has provided us over the years, and we look forward to working with you in the coming months. It was my pleasure to accompany you to South America to see first hand the circumstances DEA faces in the cocaine source countries.

There have been some improvements in our cooperative narcotics control efforts with countries in this hemisphere, notably Mexico. However, some major challenges still need to be met before we can confidently say that efforts aimed against the world's most powerful drug traffickers have been effective. The U.S. Government's efforts against these criminals have been multi-faceted.

Today's well-financed and sophisticated international narcotics traffickers are the organized crime figures of the 1990's. For over 30 years, Americans have had a view of organized crime as a group of individuals involved in extortion, loan sharking and gambling. Today, we are facing a new breed of international organized criminals whose power and influence have grown far beyond any we have seen before.

We are here today to describe for you the operations of these foreign drug syndicates and how they introduce themselves, their poison and their violence into our communities. These groups are headquartered in Colombia and Mexico, and their leaders control the vast majority of drug trafficking within the United States. There is no doubt that much of the crime that impacts communities across the United States is attributable both directly and indirectly to organizations such as the Cali Cartel, and the groups within the Mexican Federation—the Sonora Cartel, the Tijuana Organization, the Gulf Cartel and the Juarez Cartel.

The relationship of these foreign drug organizations with crime in our communities was clearly demonstrated in May of this year when arrests, made as a result of the investigation known as Operation Zorro II, clearly indicated the domination of drug trafficking in America by the groups in both Colombia and Mexico. Their handiwork that began in the boardrooms in Cali ended in cities and towns as varied as Chicago, Illinois and Richmond, Virginia. These criminal syndicates employed hundreds of Colombians, Mexicans and Americans to transport and distribute their drugs throughout our country. This case is historic because it clearly identifies the absolute dominance of the groups in the cocaine trade in the United States. Zorro II also demonstrated that with a joint effort of the DEA, FBI , U.S. Attorneys, Criminal Division and other Federal, state and local law enforcement agencies, we can be successful by attacking the command and control functions of the drug syndicates. More importantly this strategy combined with continued cooperation allows us to be successful all along the seamless continuum of the drug trade, effectively dismantling the entire network from Cali and Sonora to Aurora, Illinois.

Zorro II is particularly important because for the first time we dismantled not only the U.S. infrastructure of a Colombian organization producing the cocaine, but also that of the organization from Mexico that provided the transportation. During the course of this eight-month investigation, law enforcement officers coordinated and shared information gleaned from more than 90 court-authorized wiretaps. The operation involved 10 Federal agencies, and 42 state and local agencies across the country, and 10 U.S. Attorneys' offices. As a result of the operation, we seized over $17 million and almost 5,600 kilos of cocaine, and arrested 156 people. In Aurora we conducted four court-authorized wiretaps and arrested 12 subjects, who the organization sent to Chicago to control their wholesale distribution cell.

The Cali Cartel and the Situation in Colombia

Fifteen days ago we marked the first anniversary of the beginning of the end of the Cali Cartel. On June 9, 1995, Gilberto Rodriguez Orejuela was arrested by the Colombian National Police, setting off a chain reaction which culminated in the arrests of six of the seven top Cali cartel leaders in the last year. As we note this anniversary, we should assess where we are today in the international drug trade, and what our prospects are for success in the long term, as we work with other nations to eliminate major drug trafficking organizations. DEA continues to work closely with officials in foreign countries to target the highest levels of the international drug trade in Colombia, Mexico, Peru, Bolivia and other countries where drugs are produced and transported.

The significance of last year's arrests of six of the seven top leaders of the Colombian cartel cannot be overstated. Masterful police work on the part of the Colombian National Police, working with DEA and other U.S. Government agencies, led to these arrests, which represent the most serious blow to international drug trafficking in history. During the months following these arrests, the world learned how influential these traffickers really are within the Colombian Government and Colombian institutions. Dating back to the first series of raids in Cali in 1991, and in particular after the three Cali principals arrests in 1995, thousands of key documents depicting the Cali Cartel's financial empire have been seized.

The Cali Cartel had operated with virtual impunity for the past 15 years. Their influence was as widespread as their drug distribution networks. From their Cali headquarters, cartel leaders ordered assassinations within the United States and directed business transactions around the world through phone and fax communications. It is critical that law enforcement continue the pressure on the remainder of the Cali infrastructure to insure its total demise.

I can illustrate how the cocaine controlled by the Cali Cartel is affecting major American cities, such as Chicago. Let me tell you about the Gangster Disciples and their chairman, Larry Hoover. The Gangster Disciples is a well-organized street gang with an estimated 30,000 members in the Chicago area, of which 9,000 are prison inmates. The gang's nationwide membership is approximately 100,000. The gang has an extreme propensity toward violent assault, robbery and murder. Of Chicago's 650 murders from 1990 to 1994, Gangster Disciple members were involved in 43% as either victims or perpetrators.

Investigation revealed that this gang is involved in money laundering, murder, and the distribution of cocaine. The cocaine that fueled this violent gang and its reign of terror on the city of Chicago is traceable to the drug lords in Colombia. Two members of the Cali cell who were supplying the gang with cocaine, were arrested in 1994 in possession of 98 kilos of cocaine and approximately $400,000 in cash.

Larry Hoover, the gang chairman, led the Gangster Disciples from inside state correction facilities that have housed him since a 1993 murder conviction. The Chicago news media have likened Hoover to Al Capone and Pablo Escobar. Hoover is currently serving a 150-200 year sentence for murder. Despite his incarceration he received $100,000 to $200,000 a week from a "street tax" imposed on drug sales and money laundering.

Last August law enforcement officers from DEA as well as state and local agencies arrested 39 gang members, including Hoover, several of the gang's top leaders—known as board members and governors—and one Chicago police officer. Hoover has been charged with violating federal statutes that include conspiracy and controlling a Continuing Criminal Enterprise. The first eight defendants were convicted last March. Two additional trials are scheduled for later this year.

As I noted earlier, the Cali cartel, which fashioned itself after the Silician Mafia and the La Cosa Nostra, became far more sophisticated and successful than its predecessors. However, in the transition stage since the Cali Cartel arrests, we have seen the same patterns of violence we observed in the La Cosa Nostra when the families fought to take over territory or fill a vacuum of power from fallen family leaders. A recent incident illustrating this point occurred in Cali when William Rodriquez-Abadabia, the son of Miguel Rodriguez-Orejuela, was wounded and six body guards killed during an ambush.

This trend is likely to continue with the increasing sophistication among the trafficking groups from Mexico, the remnants of the Cali cartel and the young violent groups emerging in Colombia as they battle to increase their control of cocaine production, transportation and distribution networks.

Complicating the Colombian situation is the very high purity of Colombian heroin for sale on the streets of major American cities. This heroin is relatively cheap, compared to that available from other worldwide sources, with a purity as high as 90% in some cases. The Colombian traffickers are utilizing well-established cocaine distribution networks to distribute heroin. By underpricing Southeast Asian and Southwest Asian heroin traffickers by as much as $20,000 to $30,000 per kilogram, these Colombian traffickers have established a substantial share of the market in the northeast corridor of the U.S. and appear poised to expand their markets in other major U.S. cities.

How did these criminals from Colombia gain such enormous power and wealth? They began in the early 1980's to monopolize the cocaine trade in the United States. The syndicates in Colombia realized the way to maximize profits was to control the product from manufacture to wholesale distribution. To that end, the Cali Cartel developed a sohpisticated, disciplined, and compartmentalized cell system for their entire criminal operational structure. The Cali drug bosses were able to combine the business acumen of a ***Fortune*** 500 company with the cunning and violence of terrorist organizations.

Further, they realized it was necessary to dominate crop production, as well as wholesale distribution. Both the Cali and Medellin Cartels struck deals with traffickers in Peru and Bolivia to buy coca leaf from peasants, process it into cocaine base and ship it to Colombia for further processing into cocaine hydrochloride (HCl). Peru and Bolivia are by far the largest producers of coca leaf in the world and over 80% of the cocaine consumed in the world is controlled by the syndicates in Colombia.

The Source Countries

Allow me to take a few moments to describe the importance of "source countries" in the global drug trade. The coca leaf, harvested in Bolivia and Peru, is processed into a pasty substance known as cocaine paste and then flown into Colombia where the paste is converted into cocaine HCl powder, packaged and shipped by the Colombian cartels to Mexican transportation organizations. In Peru and Bolivia counternarcotics actions are having a significant impact on coca processing and transportation. As a result the drug trafficking situation is now changing dramatically.

Until about five years ago, Peruvian drug traffickers like those in Bolivia were producing cocaine paste that was refined to cocaine base in large, well equipped labs located in remote jungle areas. Many of these labs were built and financed by the Colombian cartels. These efficient operations required many workers, running water, large supplies of chemicals and electrical power to operate the equipment necessary for large scale production. They were expensive for the traffickers to operate and provided law enforcement with excellent targets of opportunity. Counterdrug operations conducted in the early 1990's by the the National Police, aided by DEA, successfully targeted these massive conversion labs in Boliva and Peru, forcing the traffickers to abandon these large operations in favor of smaller, more mobile, laboratories in remote locations to reduce their losses and the risk of detection.

At the same time, law enforcement authorities, with DEA support, took aim at the traffickers' preferred method of transporting cocaine base from the mountainous jungles of Bolivia and Peru to the cartel operations in Colombia. Law enforcement efforts against this "air bridge" have forced traffickers to abandon the air route, develop alternative transportation routes, and resort to more time consuming, riskier transportation over land and water.

To avoid further disruptions to their processing operations due to the increased time and risk involved in land and marine transportation to Colombia, Bolivian and Peruvian traffickers are now beginningto refine cocaine base into cocaine HCl and distribute it directly to Mexican transporters and buyers themselves, thereby circumventing Colombian middlemen and increasing profits. Although they are not nearly as organized, powerful or wealthy as the groups in Colombia and Mexico, their potential for growth to that level is enhanced due to the increased profits that accrue to them. We are closely monitoring this disturbing trend.

Colombian drug organizations still play a part in Bolivian and Peruvian cocaine production, but there is increasing evidence that traffickers from Mexico, Peru, Brazil, Chile, Paraguay and Argentina are playing a larger role in Bolivian cocaine trafficking. Concurrently the influence of Colombian traffickers appears to be decreasing. The number and stature of Bolivian and Peruvian trafficking appears to be increasing sharply.

Meanwhile, the Government of Bolivia has enacted laws to control and regulate essential chemicals for the cocaine conversion process in Bolivia. To address the change in trafficking operations, Bolivian counterdrug police have successfully implemented these laws, made several large seizures of precursor chemicals and, with our assistance observed a change in the trends in trafficking of these chemicals. For example, cocaine base and HCl processors have begun to use substitute or reconstituted chemicals whenever possible.

On to Mexico

In order to appreciate the magnitude of Mexico's role in the international drug trade, it is important to understand that approximately 70% of the cocaine available in the United States transits Mexico. Organized criminal drug syndicates in Mexico are versatile and well-established, having been engaged in heroin, marijuana and cocaine trafficking for the past 30 years. During the late 1980's Cali traffickers turned to transportation groups in Mexico to assist them in smuggling their multi-ton loads of cocaine into the United States. This change in modus operandi was due in large part to successful enforcement and interdiction operations in south Florida and the Caribbean. Smuggling groups in Mexico were a natural choice for the Cali leaders, since they had been smuggling heroin and marijuana across the Southwest border since the late 1960's. Early on, the Mexican transportation groups were paid $1,000 to $2,000 per kilogram for their services. They would receive the cocaine in Mexico from a Colombian transportation group and smuggle it in to the United States and turn it over to a Colombian distribution cell.

In the early 1990's they reached an agreement with the Cali criminal bosses to receive payment for their smuggling services in cocaine. The Mexican smugglers began receiving up to half of every shipment of cocaine they transported. This new arrangement had the immediate effects of significantly increasing the Mexican traffickers' profits and necessitated the expansion of their own distribution networks in the United States.

As I previously mentioned, Zorro II gave an insightful look at the success and sophistication of these new distribution cells controlled by the members of the Mexican Federation. What we saw were parallel Colombian and Mexican distribution organizations with sophistcated operational structure, controlling wholesale distribution of cocaine in a wide variety of locations throughout the United States, receiving their cocaine from the same Mexican transportation group which was supplied by Cali traffickers.

The Mexican Federation

There are four major groups from Mexico under the umbrella of the Mexican Federation, an organized crime group which operates in many parts of Mexico.

The Tijuana Organization is headed by the Arellano Felix brothers, Benjamin, Francisco and Ramon. It is headquartered in Tijuana, Baja California Norte. This group controls smuggling across the border to California and is among the most violent of the Mexican organizations and has been connected by Mexican officials to the killing of Cardinal Juan Jesus Posadas-Ocampo at the Guadalajara Airport in 1993. During 1994, this group was engaged in a turf battle over methamphetamine territory in San Diego. Twenty-six homicides were committed during one summer as rival groups battled over trafficking regions.

Benjamin Arellano Felix was indicted on May 2, 1989 in San Diego on charges of operating a continuing criminal enterprise which involved the importation and distribution of cocaine. Arellano Felix is frequently seen in Mexico and has never been arrested on these charges. Francisco Rafael Arellano Felix, his brother, was indicted in San Diego in 1980 for possession and conspiracy to possess cocaine.

The Sonora Cartel is headed by Miguel Caro Quintero, and operates out of Hermosillo, Agua Prieta, Guadalajara and Culican, as well as the Mexican states of San Luis Potosi, Sinaloa, and Sonora. Rafael, Miguel's brother, is in jail for his role in the killing of DEA Special Agent Enrique Camarena in 1985. The Sonora Cartel has direct links to the Colombian cartel and operates routes into California, Arizona, Texas and Nevada. Miguel Caro Qunitero was indicted in Arizona for shipping two tons of cocaine from Mexico to Arizona, and he has been indicted twice in Colorado. He continues to be a fugitive.

The Juarez cartel is headed by Amado Carillo Fuentes, the most powerful figure in the Mexican drug trade. His organization is linked to the Rodriguez Orejeula organization in Cali, and has family ties also to the Ochoa brothers in Medellin, Colombia. For many years, this organization ran transportation services for the Cali cartel and used aircraft including 727's to fly drugs from Colombia to Mexico. He also used to move drugs from regional bases in Guadalajara, Hermosillo and Torreon. Carillo Fuentes has been indicted in Dallas and Miami, and has been a fugitive for eight years.

The Gulf Group was headed by Juan Garcia Abrego and is based in Matamoros, Tamualipas State. It distributes cocaine in the

United States as far north as Michigan, New Jersey and New York. DEA has reports that this organization smuggled in excess of 30 tons of cocaine into the United States. Humberto Garcia Abrego, Juan's brother, was arrested in October, 1994 by Mexican authorities. Juan Garcia Abrego, one of the FBI's Ten Most Wanted, was arrested on January 14, 1996. After his arrest, Mexican authorities worked quickly to expel Abrego to the United States to face charges of conspiracy to import cocaine and the management of a continuing criminal enterprise.

The capture of these powerful drug traffickers, and the dismantling of their organizations operating on both sides of the border are top priorities of the Drug Enforcement Administration.

Methamphetamine

Traffickers from Mexico are also heavily involved in methamphetamine production and trafficking, the devastating effects of which are spreading across our country. Methamphetamine is a very potent and toxic drug. The common thread that runs throughout the methamphetamine trade is violence. From binge users to manufacturers to wholesale and retail distributors, violence is attendant to all aspects of the methamphetamine trade.

Methamphetamine has become a serious law enforcement and health problem, especially within the last three years.

Methamphetamine production and trafficking were previously confined to the West Coast where outlaw motorcycle gangs were responsible for the bulk of the methamphetamine available in the United States. Traffickers from Mexico have now taken over methamphetamine in the U.S., including manufacturing operations, distribution, and in some cases even obtaining the necessary chemicals from Asia and Europe, all to maximize their profits.

Methamphetamine seizures along the U.S.-Mexico border rose from 6.5 kilograms in 1992 to 665 kilograms in 1995. Previously, enormous amounts of ephedrine, an essential ingredient in methamphetamine production, were shipped to Mexico. In an 18-month period between June, 1993 and December, 1994, approximately 170 metric tons of ephedrine was diverted from the international commercial trade to Mexico. This amount of ephedrine could be used to produce an estimated 119 metric tons of methamphetamine. Effective controls are being implemented in an attempt to control the availability of ephedrine and other essential chemicals.

The impact of methamphetamine trafficking and its use has been devastating to many cities and rural counties in the United States in areas as diverse as Iowa, Georgia and Florida. Methamphetamine deaths have risen dramatically in cities such as Phoenix, Los Angeles, San Francisco and San Diego. In Phoenix deaths have jumped 510% between 1992 and 1994. While methamphetamine use has not yet reached epidemic proportions in the Chicago area, its use is steadily spreading eastward.

Another tragic aspect of methamphetamine production has been its impact on the environment. Many of the labs are often operated by individuals who have direct links to organizations based in Mexico, and these labs pose a hazard to both law enforcement officers investigating them, and also to residents in communities surrounding the labs.

Cooperation with the Government of Mexico

Both President Zedillo and Attorney General Lozano are committed to fighting narcotics and eliminating major drug trafficking organizations. They are cognizant of the negative consequences that unchecked cocaine trafficking has had in Colombia, and they are working to ensure that traffickers in Mexico do not become as well-entrenched and powerful as they have in Colombia during the past decade.

There are many obstacles facing the President and the Attorney General in their efforts, but despite these, some important steps are being taken by the Mexican Government to address problems created by major drug trafficking organizations. President Zedillo pledged in his State of the Union address that Mexico would pass comprehensive organized crime legislation. The Mexican legislature has passed, subject to the approval of the Mexican States, organized crime legislation authorizing, for the first time, a witness protection program, judicially-approved electronic surveillance, undercover operations, conspiracy prosecutions, controls on the production of precursor chemicals and an interagency financial investigative unit, as well as providing for asset seizure and forfeiture for the proceeds of crimes covered by the Organized Crime Bill.

The Mexican Government has recently criminalized money laundering under the penal code. This new provision in effect since May 14, 1996 provides for sentences for violation of its terms, as well as a 50% enhanced sentence when the violator is a government official in charge of the prevention, prosecution, or investigation of money laundering offenses. In addition, the public official likewise is barred from public office for a period equal to the sentence.

Additionally, asset seizure and forfeiture provisions of the organized crime legislation have been approved by the Mexican legislative branch, and are awaiting approval from the Mexican states. These provisions cover the forfeiture of assets, if it is determined that they were amassed as a result of organized crime or criminal activity.

The Mexican Government has also reformed its penal code to modernize provisions against the smuggling of precursor chemicals. Additionally, in March, 1996, the Mexican Government's Public Security Law became effective. This law helps Mexico professionalize law enforcement throughout the country, and includes provisions which direct law enforcement agencies to conduct comprehensive background investigations,

43-353 97 - 2

adopt a code of ethical behavior and rotate personnel to help minimize corruption.

Cooperation between the United States and the Government of Mexico is improving. However, it is imperative for the Government of Mexico to arrest and incarcerate all the major traffickers who are significant players in the global drug trade. While the Government of Mexico has made some important improvements in their legal and penal codes, and has worked more cooperatively with the United States in recent months, some endemic problems, such as corruption and the enormous influence of the major traffickers, continue. Within the last several months, three top former law enforcement officials from Tijuana have been assassinated. These killings are indicative of the impunity with which the Mexican crime syndicates feel they can operate and consistent with the intimidation and narco-terrorist methods of the Cali and Medellin Cartels.

Conclusion

We would like to thank you again for the opportunity to testify at this hearing, and hope we have left you with a clear understanding of the drug trade in the United States. Most importantly, I want to emphasize that the drug trade is a seamless continuum—from the source countries to the streets of our cities and towns and is totally controlled by the drug barons in Colombia and Mexico. And to be successful against these powerful syndicates, we have to apply our resources all along that continuum from the growing regions of Bolivia and Peru to the syndicates' distribution cells that exist throughout the United States. I would be happy to answer any questions.

Mr. SOUDER. Thank you very much. Your testimony will be entered into the record without objection, so ordered. Generally speaking, we have a 5-minute rule in Congress. We're extending that a little longer here, but always feel free to summarize your testimony because we will have that in the written record. That way we can ask some questions and interact too. Mr. Morgan.

Mr. MORGAN. Thank you, Congressman Souder and Chairman Hastert. It's my pleasure to be here and representing the Drug Enforcement Administration in the Chicago Division, of which Indiana is a large part.

To tie in some of the things that Mr. Chretien said to you today, I'd like to show you a slide of the investigation the DEA and several other agencies, Federal, State and local just concluded a couple months ago. It was called Zorro II. Although neither Fort Wayne nor any other city in Indiana is actually named on there, this investigation affected Indiana. What it showed DEA and, I think, most law enforcement, was that the Mexican transporters of these drugs working in conjunction with distributors brought cocaine in tremendously large quantities into this country. This investigation resulted in the arrest of 136 individuals and over 12,000 pounds of cocaine was seized around the country.

In addition, we seized total assets valued at over $17 million. This was just one investigation that lasted roughly about a year. What it really showed us was that Mexican and Colombian traffickers were working solidly together. But it also showed a divergence that the Mexican traffickers had their own system down, their own sales down, just as the Colombian distributors had theirs down.

This investigation, and I'll show you another slide, to show you how this came into the Chicago area. And when I say Chicago area, I would be remiss in saying, there was, more than likely, a lot of that cocaine that got into Indiana and northeastern Indiana. But what this showed us, through various wiretaps that we had in Chicago and all of these cities named, actually, was where the divergence of where this cocaine was coming from as well as how it got to areas of Indiana, Illinois, and as far down as Rocky Mount, NC, where information led us to seizures in that small town of 30,000 people.

Craig has also mentioned about the methamphetamine problem, as you and Congressman Hastert have also mentioned, I think although DEA intelligence is not showing an epidemic type problem with methamphetamine in the Fort Wayne area, several communities close by do have a problem with it. But I do think that Indiana's problem with methamphetamine right now is centered more in southern Indiana. This again, as Mr. Chretien said, is an emerging problem that's kind of going off the map as far as use because it is cheaper than cocaine.

The use of methamphetamine and the hideous nature of this drug is unknown to a lot of the American public, and particularly our teenagers. We need more education for the teenagers, not just for teenagers but pre-teenagers for that matter, on the effects of this drug, which I don't think are known at this time in large measures. One of the things that we see in DEA, when we do see the clandestine lab that's manufacturing methamphetamine, is that the chemicals that are used to produce this drug, once they are finished with it and the methamphetamine is produced, basically you have a hazardous wastesite when this laboratory gets finished producing.

We spent tremendous amounts of money, and I think DEA expenditures over the last fiscal year were over $7 million to clean up these hazardous wastesites from these chemicals that were left. It also gets into the springs and drinking water supplies where they don't have the correct and proper way to dispose of these chemicals, they just dump them out the back door or whatever and it gets into the, particularly the drinking water of the areas.

Again, Fort Wayne does not have a particular problem in that regard. One final thing I'd like to touch on is the gang situation as we see it. Fort Wayne does have gangs. I'm sure Chief Moore will give you more details on this. But the gangs that we are encountering are nationwide, in particular the Black Gangster Disciples, which is a gang in Chicago that numbers over 30,000. It does have members here in Fort Wayne and other various communities in northeast Indiana.

What they're about is violent assault, robbery and murder. They're also involved in money laundering and of course, crack cocaine. Just last year in Chicago, we arrested two Cali Cartel members that were bringing in approximately 90 kilos of cocaine and we seized over $400,000 in cash. The gang situation, I think, is a situation that is invading more cities daily. They have invaded Fort Wayne, though not as bad as the larger cities are right now. But they see an opportunity to intimidate, to murder, to supply drugs to an area such as Fort Wayne and it's basically wide open without any regard for law enforcement actions.

In summary, I think the Fort Wayne area is blessed by having a department such as Chief Moore runs and the Sheriff's office here and the State police which are working extremely diligently to fight this war with us and with the counterparts here in Indiana. I would suggest that this effort of all law enforcement here in the Fort Wayne area is one that you and the other leaders of this community can be very proud of. I'll be happy to answer questions.

Mr. SOUDER. Thank you very much. Lt. Heck.

Mr. HECK. First of all let me thank the U.S. House of Representatives and the Committee on Government Reform and Oversight, Chairman Hastert and Congressman Souder for extending an invitation to the Indiana State Police Department to present testimony at this hearing.

The Indiana State Police is strongly committed to the war on drugs. We applaud all efforts to keep the lines of communication open between Federal, State and municipal governments.

I will attempt to outline the illegal drug situation in the State of Indiana and provide insight on specific drugs used, the effects on users, manufacture and distribution of illegal drugs, and the challenges associated with halting the supply and most importantly, the demand.

Illegal drug use in the State of Indiana is not a product of the 1990's. The problem Indiana faces actually began in Indiana long before these drugs were made illegal. From the home grown problem of "ditch weed," to eradicating marijuana crops planted in cornfields, to the sophisticated distribution routes of cocaine smugglers that originate in South America, the Indiana State Police and local law enforcement authorities fight a seemingly never-ending battle. Within the last three to four decades chemical drugs have also emerged to help compound Indiana's drug trafficking problem.

With all reports of the dangers associated with drug abuse and the numerous studies that have been done over the years, some people have not gotten the message. Many are willing to gamble with their lives by taking a strange and dangerous substance. Most illegal drug users don't know where the drugs originate, they don't know what kind of chemicals are in the drugs or who ultimately receives the money they spend on drugs.

It's similar to the prohibition era when the average person would go out and buy a bottle of bootleg whiskey. If you asked him if he was committing a crime, he would probably say, "No. I'm not hurting anyone. I'm just sitting here having a friendly drink in my home." When a person makes this kind of statement, he or she fails to realize that the money is being used to support an illegal activity. It goes directly into the war chest of people, at that time, like Al Capone, current day people, Noriega and the other cartels that were spoken about.

This one isolated act will ultimately increase crime in the city or county in which that person lives as well as places thousands of miles away. It's going to take all of us and it's going to take all of our effort to stem the flow of drugs into this country. It's going to take all of us to educate the public in hopes of eliminating the demand.

Drug abuse trends in the State of Indiana reveal an increase in the popularity of certain types of drugs, and a growing number of clandestine drug labs. Some of the fastest growing drugs in the State are methamphetamine, methcathinone, crack cocaine. LSD and heroin are also making strong comebacks in Indiana. Unfortunately, as in some consumer products, the increase of one drug does not necessarily mean the demand for other drugs will decrease.

The popularity of these drugs are for a number of reasons. On the average they are inexpensive, easy to obtain, and the demand is high. Many of these drugs are easy to produce in extremely dangerous laboratories that can be operated virtually anywhere with just a small amount of startup capital. These kinds of drugs when compared to alcohol and marijuana, a disturbing point comes to light. With alcohol, a person either has to carry bottles or cans around or go into a bar or tavern to obtain the substance.

This poses an obvious problem of underage users. Another problem is having to hide or cover up the scent of alcohol. Many times it's easily distinguished by a teacher or other person. Marijuana produces a distinctive odor whenever it is smoked. The odor is really easily detected and makes it hard to be discreet. Marijuana is somewhat easier to conceal than a bottle of liquor or a can of beer, but you can carry it in the form of homemade cigarettes or joints.

This is not the case with the drugs that have been becoming increasingly popular today. In many cases they can be transported and ingested without raising suspicion. Users can get high without lighting up, without using needles to shoot up. LSD is popular in mainly two mediums, small pills and small tabs of paper soaked in a solution containing LSD. The latter is called "blotter acid." The disturbing trends we're seeing is a resurgence in high school, middle school students using LSD.

Certain areas of Indiana are more likely to have difficulty with drugs that are popular in their region. We've seen an increase in the number of cases involving crack cocaine in the inner city areas, cities such as Indianapolis, Gary, and Fort Wayne, to name a few. Cities such as these often see an increase in their crime rate that coincides with the increase of drug use.

The use of methamphetamine is becoming popular throughout the entire State. It's important to realize that no place is safe from being affected and consequently infected by illegal drugs. Sometimes called "speed," or "crank," methamphetamine may very well become the drug of choice in Indiana. Its popularity is probably due to the fact that it can be manufactured in unsophisticated laboratories that can spring up anywhere. The profit margin is high, and the labs used to make the drugs are very easy to set up.

Methamphetamine users tend to be male between 19 and 40 years old with up to 45 percent between the ages of 20 and 29. Its use has increased among college students and young professionals involved in the club scene. In some areas it's become more popular than cocaine.

There are many methods of getting high on "meth." It can be snorted, inhaled, injected, smoked or taken orally. It can cause irritability, aggressive behavior, anxiety, hallucinations and paranoia. Abusers also have dramatic mood swings and engage in violent behavior.

In New Mexico, in the summer of 1995, the Nation was rudely awakened by a senseless murder of a 14-year-old boy that was beheaded by his father, who was high on methamphetamine. In December of last year, three children, all under the age of 4, were burned to death by an explosion and a fire inside a mobile home in California that was believed to have contained a methamphetamine laboratory.

We have noticed one constant in the drug use and trafficking patterns here in Indiana over the years. When we see a trend developing on the East or West Coasts of the United States, unfortunately we can be sure that it will only be a matter of time before it reaches Indiana. Methamphetamine can be extremely addictive, it creates a dependence and produces a withdrawal syndrome similar to that of other narcotics on the central nervous system. It does produce a longer, more intense high. Some users have been known to go on "binges" where they maintain their high for several days.

Several hours after it's used, the individual experiences a dramatic drop in his mood and energy level. The increased number of "meth" users has spawned a jump in the number of clandestine drug labs. These labs are used to make highly toxic, flammable chemicals that not only pose a threat of exploding, but they also cause serious damage when the accompanying fumes are inhaled or come in contact with the skin.

Cleanup of one of these labs, after the perpetrators have been arrested or have moved on, has become one of the most troublesome issues that law enforcement agencies are faced with today. A toxic dump site is left behind for law enforcement to clean up at the taxpayers' expense. Cleanup costs for one lab can be in the tens of thousands of dollars.

In the 1995 movie, "Outbreak," biologists dealt with an airborne virus that made it necessary for lab teams to wear airtight, full-body Nomex suits while in the area where the virus was present. When we have to send one of our people into a clandestine lab, they wear the same type equipment. Clandestine labs can be found anywhere. It's commonplace to discover the labs in someone's kitchen, bathroom, hotel/motel rooms, even in the back of a van traveling down the highway. We are all at risk because of the nature of these labs and chemicals used. Clandestine labs have caused explosions and fires. They create toxic fumes that are harmful when inhaled. Many are booby-trapped, filled with weapons, or both.

Distribution of these illegal drugs can mirror the state-of-the-art marketing and distribution techniques you might expect a "Fortune 500" corporation to use. It ranges from the everyday street sale level, all the way to sophisticated drug trafficking rings. The production of methamphetamine and other illegal drugs is only possible when the makers of these drugs are able to get the chemicals needed for production, mainly ephedrine and pseudoephedrine tablets. The best way to control methamphetamine traffic is to control the diversion of the chemicals by unlawful chemical manufacturers.

Congress struck a major blow against illicit drug producers by passing the Diversion Control Act of 1993. This act closed the loophole for single-entity ephedrine drug products. However, legislation is still badly needed for other chemicals such as Pseudoephedrine tablets. Drug traffickers have realized that many of the chemicals which produce "meth" and other drugs are unregulated in tablet form. Drug traffickers found that they couldn't buy it in bulk, they started buying Pseudoephedrine tablets.

Although legislation is good, enterprising individuals have also started using unregulated drugs to extract the chemicals they need to make the "meth." Now we're left with an additional wastesite. What can be done to combat the illegal drugs? If there was no demand, we wouldn't be here today. We need to discuss what has worked in other areas to convince young people to never try illegal drugs. Indiana has a Prevention Resource Center in Bloomington that studies drug trends across the Nation. The center notes that it is impossible to regulate a demand by legislation. We have to fight the demand by education.

A wise old police officer once told me that he never bothers to tell kids not to try drugs. He simply tells them what will happen to them and the people around them if they do. We need to change our attitudes about the drug problem in this country. We need to open our eyes and stop just wishing the problem will go away. Those are our kids that are buying and using these toxic chemicals. It's time to stop saying, "It was only." It was only a beer. It was only marijuana. It was only a small amount of cocaine or methamphetamine. If we don't act on this today we lose ground.

On behalf of the Indiana State Police Department, I would like to extend our appreciation for your valuable time and attention. Thank you.

[The prepared statement of Mr. Heck follows:]

Illegal Drug Use In Indiana

Congressional Testimony, Fort Wayne, Indiana
June 24, 1996

The Indiana State Police is strongly committed to the war on drugs. We applaud all efforts to keep the lines of communication open between federal, state, and municipal governments.

This report will outline the illegal drug situation in the state of Indiana and provide insight on specific drugs used, the effects on users, manufacture and distribution of illegal drugs, and the challenges associated with halting the supply and the demand.

Illegal drug use in the state of Indiana began long before many of these drugs were made illegal. From the home grown problem of "ditch weed," to eradicating marijuana crops planted in cornfields, to tracking the sophisticated distribution routes of cocaine and methamphetamine smugglers that originate in South America, the Indiana State Police and local law enforcement authorities fight a seemingly never-ending battle. Within the last, three to four decades, chemical drugs have also emerged to help compound Indiana's drug trafficking problem.

In spite of numerous published reports on the dangers associated with illegal drug abuse and the numerous studies that have been done over the years, some simply have not accepted the facts. Many are yet willing to gamble with their lives by taking a strange and dangerous substance. Most illegal drug users don't know where the drugs originate, they don't know what kinds of chemicals are in the drugs, and they don't know who ultimately receives the money they spend on drugs. These are three primary factors that seemingly must remain constant for organized crime to continue thriving on the sale of narcotics.

In many ways, it is strikingly similar to what occurred during the era of prohibition. The average user would go out and buy a bottle of bootleg whiskey in preparation for the weekend. If asked if his actions were criminal, he would in all probability say, "No." In his opinion, there was nothing wrong with his actions. He would probably say that he was wasn't hurting anyone, he was "just sitting there in his own home having a friendly drink." When a person makes this kind of statement, he or she has failed to realize that the money used to support an illegal activity goes directly into the war-chests of criminal leaders like Al Capone, Manuel Noriega, and countless organized crime leaders throughout the world. The actions of one illegal drug user will ultimately serve to increase crime in the city or town in which he or she lives, as well as in places thousands of miles away. It affects all of us, and it will take our combined efforts to stem the flow of illegal drugs into this country. It will also take all of us to educate the public in hopes of eliminating the demand.

Drug abuse trends in the state of Indiana reveal an increase in the popularity of certain types of drugs, and a growing number of clandestine drug labs. Some of the fastest growing illegal drugs in the state are: methamphetamine, methcathinone, marijuana, heroin, and crack cocaine. LSD is experiencing a strong comeback as well. Unfortunately, an increase in one drug does not indicate a decrease in the demand for others.

Indiana State Police Laboratory officials have identified and documented controlled substances by type and classification, and denote the following: From 1990 to 1995, identified items containing heroin were up 22%, marijuana was up 53%, methamphetamine showed an increase of 115%, and crack cocaine was up a staggering 1300%.

These drugs are becoming more popular for a number of reasons. On the average, they are inexpensive and easy to obtain, and the demand is high. Many are easy to produce in extremely dangerous clandestine laboratories that can be operated virtually anywhere with just a small amount of start-up capital.

When these kinds of drugs are compared with alcohol or marijuana, a disturbing point comes to light. With alcohol, an abuser has to either carry bottles or cans around with him, or go into a bar or tavern to get high. This poses an obvious problem for underage users. Another problem is having to hide or cover up the scent of the alcohol. A school-teacher can usually tell when a student has been drinking.

When the drug of choice is marijuana, a major problem is encountered with the distinctive odor it produces. It is not as difficult to conceal as a bottle of whiskey or a can of beer, but it is necessary to carry the drug in bags or in the form of homemade cigarettes often called "joints." At any rate, the smell of marijuana is relatively easy to detect.

This is not the case with the drugs that have become increasingly popular today. On the average, they can be transported and ingested without raising suspicions. Getting high can be accomplished without lighting up, and even without shooting up. "LSD," (lysergic acid diethylamide) is popular mainly in two mediums: small pills, and small tabs of paper soaked in a solution containing LSD. The paper is called "blotter acid." One of the most disturbing trends is the resurgence of LSD found in high schools and also middle schools.

The user places the paper in the mouth, chews or swallows it, and the LSD or "acid" is absorbed through the gastrointestinal system. Paper squares with images of cartoon characters, and artistic designs are the preferred medium because of the ease with which the drug can be concealed and ingested.

Certain areas of Indiana are more likely to have difficulty with drugs that are popular in their region. We have seen an incredible increase in the number of cases involving crack cocaine in the inner-city areas of Indianapolis, Gary, and Fort Wayne. Methamphetamine use, however, is becoming popular throughout the entire state. It is important to realize that no place is safe from being affected, and consequently infected by illegal drugs.

Methamphetamine, sometimes called "Speed," or "Crank," may very well become the drug of choice in Indiana, its growing popularity is partly due to the fact that it can be manufactured in unsophisticated laboratories that can spring up almost anywhere. The profit margin is high, and the labs used to make the drugs are very easy to set up.

Methamphetamine users tend to be male, between 19 and 40 years old, with up to 45 percent between the ages of 20 and 29. Methamphetamine use is increasing among college students and young professionals involved in the club scene. In New York, Delaware, and New Jersey, "meth," has become a major problem during all-night dance parties called "raves." In some areas, it has become more popular than cocaine.

Common methods used to get high on "meth" include snorting or inhaling. It can also be injected, smoked, or taken orally. In large doses, it causes irritability, aggressive behavior, anxiety, auditory hallucinations, and paranoia. Abusers often have dramatic mood swings, and engage in violent behavior.

In New Mexico, during the summer of 1995, the nation was rudely awakened by the senseless murder of a 14 year-old boy that had been beheaded by his father, who was high on "meth." In December of last year, three children all under the age of four were burned to death by an explosion and fire inside a mobile home in California, that was believed to have contained a methamphetamine laboratory. We have noticed one constant in the drug use and trafficking patterns here in Indiana over the years: When we see a trend developing on the east or west coasts of the

United States, we can be sure that it will only be a matter of time before it reaches Indiana.

Methamphetamine has been found to be extremely addictive. It creates dependence and produces a withdrawal syndrome similar to that of narcotics on the central nervous system. It produces a longer high, which is more intense. Some users have been known to go on "binges." "Binges" are periods of time where the drug is cooked up, and the high is maintained for up to seven days or more.

Several hours after its last use, the individual experiences a dramatic drop in mood and energy level. This is known as "crashing." The user then sleeps for three to four days. Severe depression sets in when he or she awakens and can last for days. This is when suicide becomes a major concern. Unfortunately, the easiest way to get out of this depressed state of mind, is to use the same drug that got the user there in the first place.

Methamphetamine users are often underweight, wide-eyed, and do not have much of an appetite. These young people don't realize the effects the drug has on their respiratory systems, their hearts, and their lives as a whole. A methamphetamine user can only look forward to losing his job, money, home, family, and eventually his life.

The increased popularity of "meth" users has spawned a jump in the number of clandestine drug labs. Clandestine labs are used to mix highly toxic, flammable chemicals that not only pose a threat of exploding, but may also cause serious damage when the accompanying fumes are inhaled or come in contact with the skin.

Cleanup of one of these labs, after the perpetrators have been arrested or have moved on, has become one the most troublesome issues that law enforcement agencies are faced with today. A toxic dump site is left behind for us to clean up, at the taxpayers' expense. Cleanup for just one clandestine lab site can be in the tens of thousands of dollars.

In the 1995 movie "Outbreak," biologists dealt with an airborne virus that made it necessary for the lab teams to wear airtight, full-body Nomex suits while in an area where the virus was present. When we have to send in one of our clandestine lab teams to clean up a lab site, they have to go in with the same space-like suits, complete with face mask and breathing apparatus. The chemicals used to make these potent drugs, can cause irritation of the lungs, burns on the skin, and more. Clandestine labs can be found anywhere. It is now commonplace to discover drug labs in someone's kitchen, bathroom, hotel and motel rooms; even in the back of a van traveling down the highway.

You and I are at risk because of the nature of these labs and the chemicals used. A person could take his or her family on vacation and choose a respectable hotel to stay in. How can he or she be sure there is not a drug lab next door? How could they be sure the drug makers didn't use the room they are now renting? Drug labs have been found on farms, suburban homes, mobile homes, garages, and in apartments.

Clandestine labs have caused explosions and fires. They create toxic fumes that are harmful when inhaled. Many are booby-trapped, filled with weapons, or both. Individuals who make methamphetamine are commonly referred to as "chemists" or "cooks," and their education and knowledge level can range from high school drop-outs to persons with graduate degrees in chemistry. Some learn from underground publications or apprenticeships while incarcerated.

Distribution of an illegal drug can mirror the state-of-the-art marketing and distribution techniques you might only expect "Fortune 500" corporations to use. It ranges from the everyday street sale level, all the way to sophisticated drug trafficking routes. We've even seen drug distribution follow concert tours. Recently, we were able to monitor the price of LSD in Indiana. Before the rock group "The Grateful Dead" came to Indiana, a "hit" would average about five dollars. After the "Dead" arrived in town, that same dose would only cost one dollar because the market was saturated. There are people who follow the tour from city to city, and have their suppliers "Fed Ex" them packages full of LSD.

Suppliers of methamphetamine have traditionally been motorcycle gangs. While they continue to control a smaller portion of the market, methamphetamine is primarily smuggled into the United States by the same major organizations that dominate the production and trafficking of other illegal drugs that now come in through Mexico. The heaviest traffickers of "meth" are Mexican nationals residing in Mexico and the

U.S., and operating on either side of the border. These same organizations also produce and transport large quantities of cocaine, heroin, and marijuana into the U.S. on a daily basis.

The production and trafficking of "meth," and other illegal drugs is only possible when the makers of these drugs are able to get the chemicals needed for production -- mainly, ephedrine and pseudoephedrine tablets. The best way to control methamphetamine traffic is to control the diversion of the chemicals by unlawful chemical manufacturers.

Congress struck a major blow against illicit drug producers by passing the Diversion Control Act of 1993. This closed the loophole for single-entity ephedrine drug products. However, legislation is still badly needed for other chemicals, such as: Pseudoephedrine tablets, and iodine, which is used to make hydriodic acid. Drug traffickers have realized that many of the chemicals needed to produce "meth" and other drugs are unregulated in tablet form, and have started extracting the desired chemicals from other substances.

But what can be done to combat the demand for illegal drugs? The Indiana Prevention Resource Center in Bloomington, Indiana studies trends in drug use throughout the Indiana and the United States. The center notes that it is impossible to regulate a demand by legislation. The most effective way to stop the demand for drugs is through education.

The December 1995 issue of the *Journal of School Health,* points[10] to data showing that drug abuse prevention programs can produce reductions in drug use that are both lasting and meaningful. Studies at Cornell University Medical College, and the University of Southern California reported that programs teaching social resistance skills to adolescents can reduce drug use through high school and well into young adulthood. The follow-up study at USC confirms that young adults who had been exposed to a drug abuse prevention program during junior high school showed a reduction in the need for treatment of drug abuse problems.

The Indiana State Police Department supports the findings of these studies and takes proactive steps to educate children accordingly. During the last 25 years, more than 25,000 students in grades 5 through 12, have been enrolled in ISP Youth Services camps. The camps are primarily designed to promote self-esteem and leadership development. However, the curriculum includes substance abuse education and team building skills. The camps are the result of a partnership between the department and local community service clubs.

Through our Youth Services camps and the ISP Youth Education and Historical Center in Indianapolis, we teach kids that most people in society don't use controlled substances. We also inform them of the dangers that drugs present. A wise old police officer once said that he never bothers telling kids not to try drugs, he simply tells them what will happen to them, and the people around them, if they do.

Second, chemicals that are used to make methamphetamine and other drugs like methcathinone need to be made tougher to obtain. More safeguards should be in place to make sure the companies making these chemicals cease from diverting them to those making illegal drugs.

Third, the Indiana State Police Department uses clandestine lab teams that are made up of personnel from every area of the state. The teams are equipped and trained to clean up labs that can potentially cause extensive damage to individuals, or the environment. There needs to be more funding for the cleanup of clandestine labs for the states. In Indiana, once the state police close down a lab, we become legally responsible for its cleanup. This can add up to tens of thousands of dollars per lab. We had six such labs to clean up last year, and the numbers are expected to go higher. Let's stay ahead of the game by making sure the funding is in place before the cleanup begins.

The Governor's Commission for a Drug Free Indiana has a program in place called "Deal With It." Deal With It is designed to increase awareness, provide access to solutions, and encourage Indiana to deal with the issues that face us all regarding illegal drug use. More information about this program can be obtained by calling (317) 232-4219. The commission produces public service announcements for television and radio spots, and distributes printed information to inform as many Hoosiers as possible about the dangers of using drugs.

Finally, we need to change our attitudes about the drug problem in this country. We need to open our eyes and stop just wishing the problem will go away. Those are our kids that are buying and using these toxic chemicals, and it's destroying their lives. We must realize that the use of any controlled substance is wrong. It will only increase if it goes unchecked. We have to stop using the phrase, "It was only..." "It was only a beer. It was only marijuana. It was only a small amount of cocaine or methamphetamine." If we do not act on this today, we lose ground. As we continue losing ground, it sometimes becomes impossible to recover. Eventually, if we don't change, we will look up one day and the whole nation will be lost. Then, it will be too late to try, too late to change, too late to stop. We simply cannot afford to let this happen.

On behalf of the Indiana State Police Department, I would like to extend to you our appreciation for your valuable time and attention. Thank you.

Lt. Jeff Heck
Indiana State Police

Mr. SOUDER. Thank you very much. Mr. Gevers.

Mr. Gevers. Thank you, Congressman Souder and Congressman Hastert. I appreciate the opportunity and the invitation to speak with you today.

Fort Wayne, Allen County and northeast Indiana have all had quite a few successes in our battle against drugs. Recently we've begun to use racketeering laws to pursue drug organizations. We've confiscated record amounts of drugs. We've seized record amounts of money and property. We have prosecuted and convicted record numbers of defendant's at both the State and Federal levels in the last several years. We have better coordinated our resources. The Allen County Drug Task Force now includes a representative from Noble County, the Northeast Indiana Drug Enforcement Team has representatives from the State Police as well as Federal agencies, and the Metrosquad which is the coordinated effort between the Chief of Police and the Sheriff here in Allen County.

We increased the numbers of agents, police officers, prosecutors and judges who deal specifically with narcotic offenses. And the newly created Criminal Justice Coordinating Council, of which I am the Chair, assembles agency heads from the Fort Wayne Police Department, the Indiana State Police, the New Haven Police Department, the ATF, FBI, U.S. attorney's office, Allen County prosecutor's office, Adult Probation, Community Corrections and Juvenile Probation, once a month to discuss this coordinated approach to crime, to share information, and to plan our future battles against the criminals. We hope, through this counsel, to make better use of our shared resources, to develop both long and short term goals and plans of action. We are encouraged to hear the Drug Enforcement Administration may soon establish a post of duty in Fort Wayne and extend an invitation for a representative of that department to join us on the counsel.

Yet, as these gentleman have pointed out already, we struggle in our battle against drugs. Northeastern Indiana continues to provide a lucrative market for dope dealers. Fort Wayne is a hub city with interstate and toll road spokes, leading to Detroit in the north, Lima and Toledo in the east, Marion and Indianapolis in the south and Chicago to the west, is a prime delivery and distribution center. Record confiscations and seizures can also mean record deliveries.

Crack, LSD, crank, cocaine, heroin and marijuana are still around. They are easily concealed, easily transported, easily obtained and readily available. And they are in demand. We may win a battle but we are losing this war. In fact, with all due respect, the war on drugs is a misnomer. We have not been fighting a war. We have been embroiled simply in skirmishes of limited engagement whose purpose has been simply containment of this problem.

To quote columnist P.J. O'Rourke, we're "not serious about the drug trouble in this country. We're not serious about the trouble causing the drug trouble. We're not serious about anything." If we truly had declared war on drugs, we would have won by now. We would have had this licked.

The National Review recently boldly stated, "The war on drugs is lost." They devoted the magazine cover to that proposition and supported it with essays from conservatives and liberals including a mayor, a former police chief, a Federal judge, a psychiatrist, a law professor, a director of a drug policy research institute and a noted political columnist.

I'm not convinced. The essayists in that article confuse war and prohibition. Just as the prohibition of alcohol failed, they argue, so the prohibition of drugs has failed. But simple prohibition of behavior does not mean that we do all we can to prevent that behavior and that we fight that war. There is the crux of prohibition's failure. We have not fought a war. We have not taken and are not taking drugs seriously. For us to succeed, we must, as a country, seriously address this issue, as I give credit to you gentlemen, you're doing here today.

We must seriously, at all levels, debate our commitment to prohibition and our commitment to this drug war. If we seriously declare a drug war, I do not advocate and will not advocate the suspension of constitutional rights nor tanks along our borders. I do, however, advocate continued agency cooperation with an end to intra-law enforcement turf battles, concrete goals, plans of strategy, the availability and use of the latest technologies for all law enforcement agencies, shared information through open communication among all agencies at all governmental levels, swift and certain justice, truth in sentencing, economic sanctions for countries of manufacture and export, the targeting of major distributor and the cooperation of citizens. First and foremost, a national pride in this fight. A pride that bridges rhetoric to action. As I mentioned before, you gentlemen are taking action by being here today.

At the same time, ought we to consider an end to prohibition? Certainly, for no serious war can be declared without an unequivocal belief in the cause. So let us seriously debate this legalization of drugs that has been eluded to. A legalization perhaps with limiting laws similar to those already in place for alcohol and tobacco. But do we, as a country, believe in the moral evil of drugs? Or do we believe, as liberals and libertarians alike, that the choice for me to be drug free is up to me, the individual?

We are on the cusp of that debate. We will join in. But I am not convinced. I want to make that very clear. I am not convinced that we should put an end to our prohibition. I'm not convinced that we will save lives through legalization. I am not convinced that the Government can sell crack cocaine any more cheaply than it's being sold now on the street. I am not convinced that drug usage is not immoral. Nor am I convinced that we cannot win a real war on drugs.

We have the ability. What we must all ask ourselves today, do we have the desire? For it is far too easy to prohibit, far too hard to prevent. It is far too hard to declare a war and far too difficult to fight it.

In northeast Indiana here we struggle, but we are fighting hard to contain. We must take drugs seriously for it is our challenge as a country and as a community to make an all out effort, as these gentlemen have already pointed out, to prohibit and prevent, to investigate and integrate, to incarcerate and to treat, just say no and to give our children alternatives. Until we fully commit we will simply contain, and that is not good enough. Thank you.

[The prepared statement of Mr. Gevers follows:]

Report From the Front Line:
Fort Wayne's Battle Against Drugs
24 June 1996
Congressional Field Hearing

Thank you, ladies and gentlemen, for the invitation and opportunity to talk with you today.

Fort Wayne, Allen County, and Northeastern Indiana have had successes in the battle against drugs. We have begun to use racketeering laws to pursue drug organizations. We have confiscated record amounts of drugs. We have seized record amounts of money and property. We have prosecuted and convicted record numbers of individuals at the state and federal levels in the last several years. We have better coordinated our resources. We have increased the numbers of officers, agents, prosecutors, and judges who deal specifically with narcotics offenses. The newly created Criminal Justice Coordinating Council, of which I am Chair, assembles agency heads from the Fort Wayne Police Department, New Haven Police Department, Indiana State Police, ATF, FBI, U.S. Attorney's Office, Allen County Prosecutor's Office, Adult Probation, Community Corrections and Juvenile Probation, once a month to discuss a coordinated approach to crime, to share information, and to plan our future battles against the criminals. We hope to make better use of shared resources to develop both short and long term goals and plans of action. We are encouraged to hear that the Drug Enforcement Administration may soon establish a post of duty in Fort Wayne and extend an invitation for a representative to join the Council.

And yet, we struggle in our battle against drugs. Northeastern Indiana continues to provide a lucrative market for dope dealers. Fort Wayne as a hub city with interstate and toll road spokes -- Detroit to the North, Lima and Toledo to the East, Marion and Indianapolis to the South, and Chicago to the West -- is a prime delivery and distribution center. Record confiscations and seizures can also mean record deliveries. Crack, LSD, crank, cocaine and marijuana are still around. They are easily concealed, easily transported, easily obtained, and readily available. And, they are in demand.

We may win a battle, but we are losing the war. In fact, the "War on Drugs" is a misnomer. We have not been fighting a war; we have been embroiled in skirmishes of limited engagement whose purpose has been simply containment.

To quote P.J. O'Rourke: "...(W)e're not serious about the drug trouble in this country. We're not serious about the trouble causing the drug trouble. We're not serious about anything." ("Taking Drugs - Seriously", Rolling Stone, November 30th, 1989).

If we had truly declared war on drugs, we would have won by now.

The National Review recently boldly stated: "The war on drugs is lost," devoted the magazine cover to that proposition, and supported it with essays from conservatives and liberals: a mayor, a former police chief, a federal judge, a psychiatrist, a law professor, a director of a drug policy research institute, and a noted political columnist. (National Review, February 12, 1996).

I am not so convinced. The essayists confuse war and prohibition. Just as the prohibition of alcohol failed, they argue, so the prohibition of drugs has failed. But simple prohibition of behavior does not mean we do all we can to prevent that behavior, that we fight that war.

There is the crux of prohibition's failure: we have not fought a war. We have not taken, and are not taking, drugs seriously. For us to succeed, we must, as a country, seriously address this issue. We must seriously, at all levels, debate our commitment to prohibition and our commitment to war.

If we seriously declare war, I do not advocate suspension of constitutional rights or tanks along our borders. I do, however, advocate agency cooperation with an end to intra-law enforcement turf battles, concrete goals, plans of strategy, the availability and use of the latest technologies, shared information through open communication among all agencies at all governmental levels, swift and certain justice, truth in sentencing, economic sanctions for countries of manufacture and export, the targeting of major distributors, the cooperation of citizens, and a national pride in the fight, a pride that bridges rhetoric to action.

In short, let us approach the fight as we did World War II, not Vietnam.

At the same time, ought we to consider an end to prohibition? Certainly, for no serious war can be declared without an unequivocal belief in the cause. So let us seriously debate the legalization of drugs with limiting laws similar to those already in place for alcohol and tobacco. Do we, as a country, believe in the moral evil of drugs? Or do we believe, as liberals and libertarians alike, that the choice for me to be drug free is up to me, the individual?

We are on the cusp of the debate. Let us join in.

I am not convinced that we ought to end our prohibition. I am not convinced that we will save lives through legalization. I am not convinced that the government can sell crack cocaine any more cheaply than it is being sold now on the street. I am not convinced that drug usage is not immoral. Nor am I convinced that we cannot win a real war on drugs.

We have the ability. Do we have the desire? It is far too easy to prohibit and far too hard to prevent. It is far too easy to declare war and far too hard to fight it.

In Northeast Indiana we struggle, but we are fighting hard to contain. We must take drugs seriously. We are ready to declare war -- and win!

Mr. SOUDER. Thank you very much. Chief Moore.

Chief MOORE. On behalf of the Fort Wayne Police Department, I want to thank you, Congressman Souder and Chairman Hastert, for allowing us the opportunity to provide some update on where we have come from since 1988 in particular. As a still wet-behind-the-ears police chief in that year, the U.S. attorney for the Northern District in Indiana, James Richmond, came into town in June and promptly, before a group of 149 narcotics officers, said that Fort Wayne was the crack capital of the State of Indiana. That was a wonderful title for him to give us.

Since that time, we have been battling very, very vigorously to make sure that that title does not stick in this city. Another thing I would like to preface is to give some thanks here because not only has the Fort Wayne Police Department been fighting vigorously in this effort, but I would like to thank the administrators and officers and special agents of the Allen County Police Department and the State Police, Federal Bureau of Investigation, the Bureau of Alcohol, Tobacco and Firearms, and the Internal Revenue Service and also our friends at the DEA that visited for some length of time last summer very significantly and I will comment on that later.

One of the tasks that was provided to me was to try to provide some information, some comparison on where we have been and where we are going. In 1988, if I was to stick my head in the door of our vice narcotics division officer and say, "How many drug houses are we up to now?" because we do make every effort to track those numbers, it would not have surprised me to hear the number 175. I say that in hindsight. That was very surprising in 1988, that the crack cocaine epidemic and those marketing crack in our city had gotten such a strong foothold.

When I asked our coordinator of our Drug House Ordinance today, "On any given month, how many drug houses are reported," he may say 60, he may say 40, he may say 70, depending on the month. That tells me, at least incrementally, that we are making some strides, small as they may be.

What have we done and what works? If there were two watch words in the drug fight at the local level, Congressman Souder, I would say this. They would have to be flexibility and it would have to be diversity. One of the things that we continue to find is that as we make or take some enforcement strategy at any given time in this battle, it will shortly be countered. Down the road, 6, 7 months, there will be some countering efforts on the part of those that market drugs in our city.

Recognizing that as a fact, what have we done since 1988. What I can tell you is this. We've attempted to be flexible, to be diverse in these ways. In 1990, we established a school drug incident program. A liaison, one of our officers of the Fort Wayne Police Department, went to all high schools and middle schools inside the jurisdiction of the city limits of Fort Wayne. The concept here is to take one officer out of our narcotics division and have that officer in such a position that the routine handling of any narcotics found in our schools would meet with all legal protocols so that if the individual had to be taken to court, there is a standard method of doing that.

I can pose a chart for you and your staff that will show the years through 1995, how many young people have been taken into custody based upon primarily the use of the in-school drug program. In the early years, in the late 1980's, into the early 1990's, when Detroit, MI was one of our prime source cities, there was a working relationship that was developed where there were numerous bus interventions by the Fort Wayne Police Department.

In fact, after approximately 4 to 5 years of that operation, we will now interdict busses on a periodic basis and we have been told that we have dropped bus ridership out of Detroit by 30 to 40 percent based upon our interdiction efforts.

In addition to that, we forged new partnerships with those involved in the package industry, and air freight industry so that if anything suspicious appears to be coming in through that mode of travel, then our narcotics division officers are routinely contacted. Again, trying to be diverse, trying to be flexible.

Something at the local level that I think bears some note, I think it bears some examination for possible recognition is the Fort Wayne Drug House Ordinance. In the fight against drugs, one of the things that has come very prominent at the local level is this, our officers may go through great lengths to engage in securing search warrants. We will serve those search warrants very vigorously. We may confiscate a certain amount of drugs and take the dealer to jail.

Prior to this ordinance, it was not uncommon to have some member of that drug dealer's organization to step right in, fill the void, and actually begin selling drugs from the same location within hours. Today, based upon this ordinance that mandates that the police department can do certain types of surveillance, an ordinance that mandates certain notices to landlords and it mandates the police department to work with responsible efforts.

Last year we were responsible by using this ordinance in effectively closing down approximately 110 locations in Fort Wayne. Another major effort that I believe bears some scrutiny with people is our community anti-narcotics team. This is a five phase approach where we engage in targeting, surveillance, intensive undercover enforcement, saturation of controls and a wind down maintenance period that is targeted geographically amongst hardened areas of our city.

I'd like to conclude though by just talking briefly about multijurisdictional efforts. We are obliged to fight drugs locally. Drugs have such a horrible impact on the local community and we are obviously committed to doing just that. But one of the other ways that we have to fight drugs is to join forces with prosecutors and other area law enforcement personnel and our Federal colleagues to try and interdict and stop the flow of narcotics across our city borders.

Within the last year, there have been seven noteworthy cases. In June 1995, in cooperation and having technical assistance from the Drug Enforcement Administration we concluded the Fred Bledsoe investigation yielding over 1 kilogram of cocaine.

August 1995, in conjunction with our friends in the ATF, we concluded the Brent Scott investigation. This was an 8-month investigation yielding approximately $78,000 in cash.

In August 1995, again working in conjunction with the DEA and the Metropolitan Enforcement Group of Southwest, Illinois, the Jeirmal Walker/Shaft Jones investigation was concluded netting 5.25 kilograms of cocaine coming into the city of Fort Wayne.

A very extensive multijurisdictional task force in North East Indiana Drug Enforcement Team, who's Federal players include ATF, FBI and in this case the IRS, were involved in a multi-year investigation involving one Michael Wayne Mitchell.

September 5, 1995, and in my testimony I would alert your staff to change the last name of Martinez to the last name Diaz, D-I-A-Z. The Salvador Diaz investigation netted 156 grams of heroin, 7.3 pounds of marijuana and over $13,000 in cash. This was worked in conjunction with the DEA.

December 1995, the James Mueller/Rafael Mora investigation, again working in conjunction with the DEA, 100 grams of cocaine, 450 grams of marijuana and $24,000 in cash was seized.

January 1996, working with the Missouri State Police and the DEA an investigation of one Michael Marchbanks yielded 160 pounds of marijuana and over $160,000 in cash.

This type of interaction is what I think helps point to the fact that by working together and having the Federal presence in the city of Fort Wayne, we are going to be far more effective than trying to take scarce local resources and stretching them to the point that perhaps we could never have approached some of the dealers that I have just mentioned.

Your work, the work of other city officials, Senators here and trying to secure a DEA office is a very welcome relief. We think it is one more piece to our puzzle here in trying to keep this bite on crime.

On behalf of the Fort Wayne Police Department, I want to thank you both for being here and allowing us to present this testimony.

[The prepared statement of Mr. Moore follows:]

SUBCOMMITTEE ON NATIONAL SECURITY,
INTERNATIONAL AFFAIRS
and CRIMINAL JUSTICE

"Report from the Front Line:
Fort Wayne's Battle Against Drugs"

It is a pleasure to address the members of this Subcommittee on an issue that continues to negatively impact our communities, to demand more of our policing resources, and to contribute to general rates of criminality. Since the last visit of a Congressional Subcommittee to our City to receive testimony regarding this topic, the efforts of our citizens and the criminal justice community have been expanded to diminish the impact of illegal drugs in Fort Wayne. While we are making limited progress, our fight is far from over. Unlike some cities our size, a stronger federal presence is needed to address higher level dealers and the international and interstate distribution of narcotics to our area. In cities such as Fort Wayne, we continue to have the opportunity to turn the corner on the menace of illegal drugs. Without the allocation of additional federal resources to our situation, the opportunity to save our City will surely slip away. Our efforts here have been diverse and innovative. Changing enforcement activities, utilizing new ideas will be the hallmark of the fight against drugs.

For the purpose of this commentary, I will focus on our ongoing enforcement efforts conducted by our agency. On the education/demand reduction side of this issue, we continue to be active in the Drug Abuse Resistance Education program (D.A.R.E.) D.A.R.E is still the foremost drug resistance education effort in our country. One need only visit a fifth grade D.A.R.E culmination to realize that the Fort Wayne Community Schools, our other school systems, and the Fort Wayne Police Department are on the right track as we reach out to the young people in our City. Similarly, speaking engagements by members of our Vice/Narcotics Division add to the education of concerned adults and parents regarding the menace of drugs. These efforts must and will continue. Every young person who chooses not to become a part of the drug subculture reduces the need to keep large amounts of taxpayer dollars devoted to the enforcement effort against drugs. These efforts are indeed vital.

ENFORCEMENT EFFORTS

Enclosed you will find a chart that details some of the performance indicators that our agency routinely tracks to partially determine the effectiveness of our Narcotics Division. For most categories shown, increases are evident from one year to the next. The men and women of this Division take their jobs very seriously. They and their colleagues in our Uniform Division are extremely dedicated to ridding our communities of the drug menace. Our mission statement references our goal of improving the quality of life in our City. The actions of our agency regarding the drug fight demonstrate our attempt to do just that . . . improve the quality of life for our citizens.

School Drug Incident Program:

This effort was established in 1990 as a method to coordinate the handling of incidents where illegal drugs were found on school property. One detective of our Narcotics Division was assigned to liaison with all middle schools and high schools in our City. This effort ensures the consistent handling of youth found in possession of drugs. Narcotics found on school property are handled pursuant to protocols that maximize the introduction of this evidence in juvenile detention proceedings. Since 1990, 465 juveniles have been detained as a result of the School Drug Incident Program. This program received the Governor's Exemplary Project Award in 1990.

Community Anti-Narcotics Team:

In 1991, street-side dealing of crack cocaine had to be thwarted. After examining the Metro Dade County Tactical Narcotics Team (TNT) plan, it was decided that our agency would implement a modified version of that plan. Our version of this plan involves five (5) phases:

Phase I - Targeting - Utilizing crime analysis data, Narcotics Division data, anecdotal data from patrol officers and information from residents of potential target neighborhoods, geographical areas of our City are targeted for intensive enforcement efforts.

Phase II - Surveillance - In this phase, undercover officers photograph and/or video areas that are particularly problematic within the target area. Attempts are made to identify suspected drug-involved individuals in the area. These people may become the focus of future investigative efforts.

Phase III - Intensive Undercover Enforcement - Using a variety of techniques, members of the Narcotics Division infiltrate the area to arrest as many drug-involved people as possible in a three to six week period.

Phase IV - Saturation Patrol - After the completion of the Phase III effort, the target areas receive additional focused, patrol resources. These patrol units saturate the area. Using existing probable cause, these officers will stop vehicular and pedestrian traffic in the target area. If evidence of illegal drug possession is found, arrests are to be made.

Phase V - Maintenance - In this phase, after six to twelve weeks of saturation patrol, patrol units are slowly withdrawn. Field supervisors monitor the area to determine if achieved results are remaining constant. If not, saturation efforts may be reinstituted.

Every implementation of CAN-Team has produced the desired results. Street-side dealing is virtually eliminated in the target areas. Arrest numbers (including traffic citations) will usually be very high, 600 to 1,000+ in any four to six month effort. Some displacement does occur, but never at a 100% level.

In the past two years, we have modified this plan to rely more on saturation patrol and less on intensive undercover enforcement.

This was a result of observing fewer individuals willing to sell crack cocaine at street-side.

This has been a very effective program for dealing with the retail sale of illegal drugs. We are currently in the targeting phase of our 1996 effort. For the first time since 1991, we are exploring geographical areas outside of southeastern Fort Wayne.

<u>Bus Interdiction, Package Interdiction, Air Freight Interdiction</u>:

Through cooperative arrangements with the bus company and various package and air freight businesses in our area, suspicion of the movement of illegal drugs through these means of transportation can be routinely investigated. Using narcotic detections canine handler teams, luggage and packages can be easily checked to confirm or deny these suspicions. If an alert is obtained, our courts will normally issue a search warrant based upon the alert of our dogs. This may further investigations to the point of controlled deliveries to the intended recipients of these packages.

When the Detroit drug connection to Fort Wayne was so predominant in the late 1980s and early 1990s, our bus interdiction efforts ultimately dropped ridership from Detroit by 30% to 40%. Bus interdiction efforts have to be undertaken only on a periodic basis at this time.

Because of the ever changing methods of drug distribution, these enforcement efforts must remain part of the overall strategy to combat narcotics.

DRUG HOUSE ORDINANCE

As the number of search warrants served has increased over the years, once the dealer has been released on bail, many would return to the same location within hours of their arrest. On other occasions as the dealer was being carted off to jail, another member of the dealer's organization would immediately begin the sale of narcotics again. Relief to the community under these conditions was very short lived. Recognizing that many of the properties from which crack cocaine was sold were rental properties, an effort was undertaken to provide more relief to communities faced with this problem.

Councilman Archie Lunsey and Councilwoman Rebecca Ravine drafted and helped pass a local ordinance that:

(1) Mandated local police to notice landlords if suspected drug activity was occurring on their property;

(2) Mandated that landlords take eviction action should they be noticed that a search warrant had been served at their property as the result of a narcotics investigation; and

(3) Mandated that the Chief of Police work with and aid in educating landlords in tenant screening, lease development, and identifying signs of drug involvement on their properties.

The fear of law-abiding landlords and property management firms regarding this ordinance have been put to rest. A new synergy has developed between our agency and these responsible property owners. As a result of this effort, drug-involved tenants in over 100 properties were forced to move to other houses and some

43-353 97 - 3

to other cities. Some would talk about the displacement of the problem. In approximately three cases in 1995 where this ordinance was used did the same names appear. Some displacement, yes, but never at 100%. Our agency would hold this ordinance up to others as an example of an excellent tool to fight street-level dealing. From our experience, the ordinance must be managed by a full time member of a police organization. In our case, Mr. Joe Musi, a retired officer, was rehired to oversee this effort. His work has also been exemplary.

<u>OTHER MULTI-JURISDICTIONAL EFFORTS</u>

So far this document has focused on efforts at the local, retail drug dealing end of the drug fight. Eliminating the sale of illegal drugs at the street level must be done. If our communities are to be saved, resources must be expended to eliminate and arrest retail drug dealers. Yet more must be done to stop the flow of illegal drugs into the City. Wholesale dealers crossing our country's borders and state lines must be identified and brought to justice. Local resources and local authority are hard pressed to address this problem.

Our agency, like many others, has joined forces in multi-jurisdictional task force operations to address the mid-level and wholesale distribution schemes so common with illegal drugs. Over the intervening years since a Congressional Subcommittee visited our City, our agency has dedicated resources to task force operations.

We have been involved in the Allen County Drug Task Force, the Northeast Indiana Drug Enforcement Team (NEIDET), short term investigations in conjunction with the Bureau of Alcohol, Tobacco and Firearms, and most recently, we received the aid and assistance of the Drug Enforcement Administration through their Mobile Enforcement Team (M.E.T.).

I publicly must thank the administrators, officers, and special agents of the Allen County Sheriff's Office, the Indiana State Police, the Federal Bureau of Investigation, the Bureau of Alcohol, Tobacco and Firearms, and the Drug Enforcement Administration for dedicating resources to aid our City in the fight against drugs.

I hope in reviewing the performance indicator chart that you noted the increases occurring in 1995. I do not believe to be coincidence that 1995 also happened to be a year in which many of our task force involvements produced significant results. Between June of 1995 and January of 1996, our involvement with federal law enforcement agencies produced the following:

(1) June, 1995: Fred Bledsoe Investigation. Investigated for dealing cocaine leads to the seizure of cocaine, cash, one residence, one business, and one vehicle. D.E.A. provided technical and equipment assistance.

(2) August, 1995: Brent Scott Investigation. Allegations of dealing cocaine lead to the arrest of Mr. Scott, pending seizure of cash, one residence and two motor vehicles. This investigation was worked jointly with A.T.F.

(3) August, 1995: Jeirmal Walker/Shaft Jones Investigation. Investigated for conspiracy to distribute cocaine leads to their arrests and the seizure of cocaine, marijuana, and weapons, and the pending seizure of cash. This investigation developed through the initiative of the D.E.A. and the Metropolitan Enforcement Group of Southwest, Illinois.

(4) August, 1995: Michael Wayne Mitchell Investigation. Mr. Mitchell was investigated for dealing cocaine and heroin. This was a N.E.I.D.E.T. investigation and also involved the Internal Revenue Service.

(5) September, 1995: Salvador Martinez Investigation. This led to the seizure of heroin, marijuana and cash. This investigation was worked in conjunction with the Drug Enforcement Administration.

(6) December, 1995: James Mueller/Rafael Mora Investigation. These men were investigated for conspiracy with the intent to distribute cocaine. This investigation led to the seizure of cocaine, marijuana, and cash. The D.E.A. was our partner in this investigation.

(7) January, 1996: Michael Marchbanks Investigation. Working in conjunction with the Missouri State Police and D.E.A., this investigation led to the confiscation of 160 pounds of marijuana and $160,000.

The point of this chronology is that the hard work of local police officers combined with the hard work and additional resources of federal agencies can make a difference in cities the size of Fort Wayne, Indiana. When a group of hard working detectives and special agents know they have the resources to work against those distributing narcotics at or near the wholesale component of the drug distribution chain, good things can happen.

The ongoing efforts of the current federal agencies working with our agency are most appreciated. The 90-day involvement of D.E.A.'s Mobile Enforcement Team triggered many further investigations. This experience led to a renewed call that D.E.A. establish a permanent presence in our City. This request was heard by Congressman Souder and Indiana's Senators. I assure you all that we anxiously await the arrival of D.E.A.'s two agents to the City of Fort Wayne. We pledge our mutual cooperation to those special agents. We anticipate that D.E.A.'s presence, along with that of the F.B.I. and B.A.T.F. will significantly enhance our fight against drugs.

On behalf of our agency, I appreciate the time and effort of your Subcommittee in conducting your inquiry in our City. I hope that you realize that our agency is working diligently to attack the drug problem at the street level and through task force involvement, at the mid and higher level of distribution. By adding the Drug Enforcement Administration component to our existing efforts, we enhance the community's ability to eliminate or significantly diminish the impact of illegal drugs in our City.

At your leisure, I would urge you or your staff members to review the appendix material we have provided. As always, I and our agency members are prepared to respond to any additional questions.

On behalf of the Fort Wayne Police Department, thank you for your interest in this issue.

FORT WAYNE POLICE DEPARTMENT
VICE-NARCOTICS DIVISION
PERFORMANCE INDICATORS

	1990	1991	1992	1993	1994	1995
SEARCH WARRANTS	36	32	54	46	49	63
NO. ARRESTS	290	388	427	445	454	768
VALUE CONFISCATE	245,757	268,022	326,933	330,768	332,316	1,413,384
$ SEIZED	10,271	23,588	184,294	32,971	20,310	142,466
JUVENILE NARCOTICS ARRESTS	129	43	55	80	81	77

Mr. SOUDER. Thank you. I'll start in the original order with Mr. Chretien. You were, the DEA was in charge of Peru for an extended period. One of the things that we heard when we were down in Peru was that we had pressure on the Caribbean, in particular, and as we put the pressure on, the shoot down policy, and others, we drove the price down that they were paying, which has them now looking into other products. There's a certain skepticism that Mr. Gevers kind of caught about whether you can actually win a war on drugs, that, is it not, is one example? What other examples do you have that would have that would render any optimism given the fact that we're not ever likely to eliminate it completely?

Mr. CHRETIEN. Well, I agree with Mr. Gevers. I personally don't like the title "war on drugs" because it does connotate an all out effort. Aside from this, we haven't seen that much of it, frankly. But there are some successes and they're not all just attributable to our Government, frankly. The Government took a very controversial, very courageous step in formulating the policy to shoot down airplanes in violation of their air space.

I would be hard pressed for us to come up with that same procedure here for a lot of different reasons, but circumstances will—they took that step. It is having a dramatic effect on the price of coca leaf because now that the Colombian pilots are not flying these planes into Peru to pick up the cocaine base, the farmers have no product to sell. So it sits there and the price of leaf drops to where it's not profitable to grow any longer. So a lot of farmers, or opportunists who were growing coca leaves, just aren't. They've left those parts of Peru to persue another business.

The traffickers are adaptive, also. So now, as we're seeing presently, they're looking to move their product down either on rivers or by going through Brazil, which, in essence, has the same capabilities as Peru in its crime. I guess the bottom line is when we see success, we need to be prepared to jump on what we think is going to be the next method that the traffickers are going to use.

Again, we can make it very, very unprofitable for farmers to not grow the leaf and go for the long ways at fighting crime.

Mr. SOUDER. Given the fact that you said you were for treatment, education, prevention efforts and a number of things, why would you argue for more agents and dollars overseas? What's your argument for trying to go for the source countries?

Mr. CHRETIEN. Well, an example would be this, and the numbers seem relatively small. We only have several hundred DEA agents stationed overseas in these countries. They don't have the same authority that we have in the States. They act as liaisons, intelligence officers, training officers and try to sort of lead from the rear and get the host country law enforcement agencies to do the job that we should be doing.

So we really don't have one agent in this pot. We have a force multiplier of maybe 200 or 300. If he has police that he can work with effectively, that's a stroke of effectiveness. But spending $5,000, just for an example, to conduct and operate in Bolivia or Peru or Colombia for that matter, goes significantly further than that same $5,000 being spent on investigations in the States.

Also, your targets overseas, if they're targeted correctly, you're going to go against an organization that's producing tons of cocaine, whereas in the States you're going against on organization dealing with hundreds of kilos. I'm not saying that, I'm not weighing one or the other. We need to have very strong, increased enforcement action in the States. The point is that we get a lot of bang for the buck for the same amount of dollars overseas.

Mr. SOUDER. Mr. Morgan, you've been to many posts around this country and so on. Does it get harder the farther you go in the system? In other words, you start with 90 some percent in Bolivia and Peru, moving through Colombia it gets to the Mexican border and starts to fan out as it comes into this country. It's coming at you from so many different directions. Have you found that to be true? And how do you work the tradeoffs of how you go toward the source? I know one thing that came up this morning is, at what point do you try to turn, in other words, when you bust somebody in Fort Wayne, if you bust them here you can turn them on something, say out of Chicago. But if you get them in Chicago you can't get them coming at the border, if you get them at the border you can't get them back in Colombia. How do you make those kinds of decisions and do you really try to push it up to where you can get at the tons?

Mr. MORGAN. Yes, sir. We absolutely do that. When it gets to this country, whatever the drug is, when it gets into this country, you're absolutely correct, it's gone through various stages, various parts of the world to get here. Many, many people have basically taken a hand or put a hand on this supply of drugs. But what we try and do is basically what you're saying, to try and work backward from Fort Wayne to go where it came from. We do this with wire tap laws and informants and say, turning somebody that is arrested that has basically "seen the light," he or she may help themselves by working with us to get to their source.

We hopscotch backward from that source to their source to their source and we end up on the border, or across the border. As Mr. Chretien said, once we can follow that chain or that trail, if you will, back to a source country, that's where we have a great effect. By working, what I'm saying is working backward to get the sources, we find that very, very helpful and I think it not only helps the Fort Wayne area but many other smaller communities.

Mr. SOUDER. Mr. Gevers, I know this is a tough question, but with listening to the news about our jail already being packed, how do you make the decision and where do you think we're headed as far as Allen County to try and do crack downs and at the same time, where do we put the people? How do you sift through that as a prosecutor?

Mr. GEVERS. We have now, in Allen County, for all intents and purposes a drug court at least in name, if not in funding. The court, the judge in that court is making noises about developing a program that will offer treatment alternatives to particularly crack cocaine addicts, which we seem to have a large number of. I think we need to make an effort toward treatment for those people in order to cut down on the demand. As we've all said today, there will continue to be a demand but we need to address that.

And we need then to focus more on putting those dealers, the people that are out there indiscriminately selling to our children and to crack heads, behind bars and free up those beds for those individuals. It becomes a very difficult decision for any prosecutor anywhere to make when you look at the addict who is dealing just to support his or her own addiction, and what do those people need? They probably need a combination of both.

In this day of jail overcrowding, I think we need to look at alternatives to simply incarcerating those who are so addicted to a controlled substance, to get them in treatment so that they can move on with their lives.

Mr. SOUDER. We heard this morning that 75 percent of the people who committed crimes were some sort of substance abuser. Would that be similar of here?

Mr. GEVERS. I would say that probably close to 80 percent of the crime that we see is in some way related to drugs, not simply in possession or dealing, but the individuals burglarizing or stealing in order to get money for drugs, or committed some robbery while high.

Mr. SOUDER. My time is up, but I wanted to ask Chief Moore if he could elaborate a little bit more on one thing. First off, to all of your departments in general, I don't think the general public, unless they are with your officers and Federal agents, understand how unnerving it can be when you're in this type of thing, your life is always potentially on the line. There's so much money involved that anybody could throw out a gun or any number of things you've been through. Your own family has struggled with the side effects of this type of thing. I think we all commend the courage of the individuals involved.

But one of the things that always happens, I was fascinated in 1989, the debate in Detroit, they were arguing to some degree that drugs were coming into Fort Wayne because they were doing such a great job in Detroit they were squeezing it out. Others were arguing that they were doing such a poor job that they were expanding their base. Which ever way you argue it, whenever you push in one neighborhood, you squeeze out the next. Could you address how you've dealt with that phenomenon here in Fort Wayne and some of the things that you're doing with community policing and different things?

Chief MOORE. Yes, sir. I believe that it was Mr. Chretien from the DEA who talked about it not being just law enforcement's job. It's everybody's job. Early in the late 1980's, we began by encouraging citizens to use what we call a citizen's surveillance form to report information and send it in anonymously. It gave us the chance to start verifying intelligence without having to expend an officer in the field to do that. That continues to be a great source of information for us.

But the other thing we're doing, particularly in issues like our Indiana narcotics, where we will take a hardened look at the most hard hit drug areas of our city and especially when we start moving to the saturation control mode, we are stopping a lot of folks from their movement from one part of the city to another. Now we have been in this mode since 1991, and while we have changed the geographic boundaries of the areas slightly, we have also seen, as we look at the first 4 months of this year, our target area now has experienced almost an 18 percent reduction in crime over the last year, compared to where it was a year ago.

But the interesting thing is we are starting to see a slight rise in the immediately adjoining areas. With the community policing philosophy, Congressman, what we do is we interact with the citizens that we're sworn to serve and protect, verify in fact that we're seeing some sort of push out phenomena, slight displacement, then we gear up to change our method of operation. I'm talking about flexibility and diversity. We change our operation based upon our analysis, talking with our citizens, to go after where we see it reemerging.

Eventually, we will rid the city of it. Now the other part of that phenomena is that when I talk to my colleagues in the cities predominately south of here along the Interstate 69 corridor, every so often they will remark to me they have Fort Wayne drug dealers in their city. So unfortunate as that is, it also, I think is a signal to us that we have kept a certain amount of pressure on.

Mr. SOUDER. Thank you very much. I'm glad to see that Noble County has gotten involved in the task force. I think it is important to remember one thing, in the news clips that we've got in our office, in Huntington, I think, they had arrested seven over that weekend. I think four were LSD. In DeKalb County that same day 50 percent of the arrests were LSD over that weekend, which is clearly Fort Wayne is squeezing out, and the more we can work it out to the State Police and the State level. I yield to Congressman Hastert.

Mr. HASTERT. Thank you, Mr. Chairman. One of the things, Mr. Chretien, you were talking about your involvement in South American to try and stop drugs both from the source countries and interdiction. Tell me, what role does intelligence play? You started to mention it, but isn't it probably a lot easier to get information from certain sources than try to pick and choose where these drugs are coming from and where these loads are? What kind of role does that play?

Mr. CHRETIEN. It's fair to say that the most successful operations that we have conducted overseas, be it talking or providing information to a particular government about moving airplanes or maritime vessels, are intelligence driven. And you have to have a strong effective intelligence base. When I say intelligence, I mean the general sense of the word. I mean people cooperate, setting up intelligence nets, with the occurrence of the government to work with them on those efforts to identify this particular location, that particular person, there's many operations. We need to develop the strategy to attack that.

A good example that I hear often is why can't the DEA, Customs, and the FBI stop all the drugs coming in by ships? Go down to any active port, Houston, Los Angeles, Baltimore, wherever, you count the number of containers that are off loaded on ships and it's like where do you start? So you have to have intelligence. You have to have good information that will allow you to more effectively use the limited resource that law enforcement has.

Mr. HASTERT. There is new technology that is being developed to help you do that screening, but certainly if the intelligence is there, it makes the task a lot easier. I want to carry that point over to Lieutenant Heck and Mr. Gevers and Chief Moore, even to the gentleman who served on the school board, locally do you feel the State

Police and the prosecutor's office, local police force, is there a sharing of that intelligence? Is that an effective way to try to hold down drug use in your area?

Mr. HECK. I would say across the State, as these gentlemen have mentioned, across the State I think you'll find task forces working together. That seems to be the thing of the 1990's. It's a very successful tool involving the local, State and Federal officers. It's a very effective way to combat the problem. Obviously communication and cooperation amongst the different agencies are important.

Chief MOORE. I would concur with the lieutenant. No. 1, it's very cost-effective for us. The other thing I would bring before this hearing of importance is the fact that with the Mobile Enforcement Team that operates in Fort Wayne from June through October 1995, we were amazed at the amount of sharing of information that occurred from not just the DEA agents stationed here, but to the seven incidents that I spoke to earlier were based on the fact, in my opinion, that DEA intelligence developed out of Arizona, out of St. Louis, that led to identifying in one case, an individual that we did not have any information on prior to the DEA intelligence that arrived in Fort Wayne, IN. It's absolutely vital.

Mr. GEVERS. I would certainly agree with that. There are times when we all, in our various agencies and departments, get caught up with what we are doing ourselves, we are taking so many different ways. But it's amazing what we can accomplish when that intelligence is gathered. Here in northeast Indiana, that's working tremendously.

Mr. HECK. I'd like to add, embarrassingly so, a few years ago, there was, and it was part of the culture of most police agencies where you have police information, they kept it. I think it was very distractive to law enforcement in general. In fact, frankly the public doesn't want to put up with it. In the last 10 to 15 years, you see not only in law enforcement, within the intelligence, the CIA and others that I can't mention, are very much involved in sharing intelligence.

It's sort of a new era and it's the only way we're going to be effective.

Mr. HASTERT. The gentleman from the school board, we just had testimony from, as we call them in Illinois, the State attorney, from DeKalb County in Illinois, so I understand that there is DeKalb Counties all over. One of the things that they're doing is working with the school districts to be able to accumulate or to keep on a matter of record the school problems, to share those problems with local State attorney's and local police agencies. Is that happening here or not?

Mr. BROWN. There are some beginning conversations on that. I will tell you though that there is some concern from the educational standpoint when you begin to share information that you use to track students with the educational environment and it does create some problems. On one hand you want the law enforcement to be aware of activities, particular illegal activities that students may be involved in. But on the other hand, fundamentally, we want our young people to be able to receive an education and not necessarily be labeled within the classroom.

I will tell you one other thing that Fort Wayne Community Schools does do that works extremely well with the Fort Wayne Police Department, with the Prosecutor's office, and others, in attempting to share information when incidents arise, students are found to have narcotics in schools, the Fort Wayne Police Department is immediately notified. We do have an officer that is assigned the responsibility of interacting with the school system and that is a very healthy, I think, relationship between those two entities.

Mr. HASTERT. I just have one final question for Lieutenant Heck. The inner-agency task force concept, has it worked well and how do you improve it?

Mr. HECK. I'm going to answer, yes, it has worked very well. I think that the proof, and the chief and the prosecutor, I think just gave us some proof in the statistics and things they read off. If you would go around the State and around the country, for that matter, and talk to these different task forces, I think their numbers in the arrests, seizures and the like proves itself, will prove that they are a very effective way.

Mr. HASTERT. Thank you. And as chairman, I thank the panel for their very candid answers.

Mr. SOUDER. Thank you all for taking the time out of your very busy schedules to come and I know the preparation and testimony have been very helpful to us. You're dismissed.

Would the second panel come forward?

[Witnesses sworn]

Mr. SOUDER. All the witnesses responded in the affirmative. Please be seated. Let me, for the record, I need—we didn't have an original witness list. I need, Rev. Jordan, your son's name?

Rev. JORDAN. His name is Ternae Jordan, Jr.

Mr. SOUDER. And Andre, who is accompanying you?

Mr. MARTIN. Barry Martin, Jr.

Mr. SOUDER. Barry? Welcome, Barry. And then with Joe Mann?

Mr. MANN. I have Mike Douglas and Vaughn MacIlfey.

Mr. SOUDER. Well, let me introduce the panelists and then we'll begin. Rev. Ternae Jordan is the senior pastor at the Greater Progressive Baptist Church and is president of Stop the Madness Campaign. He's received numerous awards for his contribution to the Fort Wayne community, including the Martin Luther King, Jr., Community Service Award and the Fort Wayne Urban League Youth Services Award. And his son is with him, who, among other things, is a wonderful singer. We all read about it in the Saturday night newspaper. We, of course, appreciate you being here, too.

Andre Patterson serves as director of the Simba Rites of Passage Program at the Cooper Teen Center on Fort Wayne's south side. The Simba Program offers African-American boys an alternative to drugs and street violence with some interaction with adult male mentors. The program requires that participants take part in community service as well as other structured activities and expects them to take responsibility for their own actions and to live up to individual goals. They've been a wonderful addition to our community and I enjoyed meeting them out in Washington and have seen them around town. It's really great to see the enthusiasm they have, and I'm looking forward to hearing your testimony.

Joe Mann is the executive director of Abundant Life Ministries, which is an expansion and broadening of the regular jail ministry program in Allen County. It's an organization whose mission is to work with prisoners and ex-prisoners with life controlling problems. He's been ordained to the Broadway Christian Church in Fort Wayne for 8 years and serves as the Sheriff's Department chaplain as well as a member of the Fort Wayne Community Corrections Board of Directors.

Ron Davenport currently serves as the operations director of the Washington House Treatment Center. He'll be able to offer us some first hand insight into the challenges and also the successes of the work done at the treatment center and will offer us a unique perspective of Indiana's struggle against substance abuse, not only illegal substances, but alcohol abuse. Washington House has been a leader in that. Also, in some business programs, which we're going to be having some hearings on in Washington, we'll able to be a forerunner of another round of hearings we're going to do.

Thank you all for being here today. I'll ask you to go ahead with your testimony. If you could start, Rev. Jordan.

STATEMENTS OF REV. TERNAE JORDAN, STOP THE MADNESS CAMPAIGN; ANDRE PATTERSON, DIRECTOR OF THE SIMBA PROGRAM; JOE MANN, DIRECTOR OF ABUNDANT LIFE MINISTRIES; AND RON DAVENPORT, OPERATIONS DIRECTOR OF THE WASHINGTON HOUSE TREATMENT CENTER

Rev. JORDAN. Thank you, Chairman Hastert and Congressman Souder. I appreciate the opportunity in coming before you to share this testimony. Our Stop the Madness program originated in this community in 1992. In January 1992, I had the unfortunate task of funeralizing a 15-year-old young lady who had been shot in the head. The news was that she was playing Russian Roulette. I also had, at that funeral, 1,600 to 1,700 young people with looks of disbelief. They were asking the question who would be next. It didn't take very long because 3 weeks later we buried another 15-year-old who had been shot in the head playing Russian Roulette.

The same thing occurred, 1,600, 1,700 young people with looks of disbelief. A month later we buried another 19-year-old young man. During the year of 1992, we buried 12 young people, all under the age of 19, from violence in our community.

After the second funeral, the members of our congregation decided that we need to do something. So we decided that we would draw this communities attention, their focus to what was going on with our young people. We were totally convinced that violence is a language. The problem is, those of us who are hearing it are not being able to interpret what they're hearing. So on February 29, 1992, we held at Progressive Baptist Church a seminar and we entitled it, "Stop the Madness." We had over 850 throughout our community, parents, our city officials, our school officials, police chief, our mayor was there. Our public officials gathered and we heard testimonies coming from our youth.

We wanted to make sure that we had the youth group, many times they're involved in negative behavior there, so we went out and through the juvenile court system and they were there on that day. After we had the first seminar, it was so successful and we got such a positive response from the community that we decided in May 1992, to have another one. At that time, a young man offered us the use of his summer camp and that summer of 1992, we were able to work with 216 kids at a week-long summer camp.

We had 9 weeks. We dealt with issues that were relevant to young people, self-esteem, motivation, staying away from drugs, staying away from gangs and those kinds of activities. And thus, Stop the Madness was created.

The mission of Stop the Madness is that, Stop the Madness exists for the purpose advancing creative solutions for ending the needless violence which has come to characterize so much of American life and interpersonal interactions, especially among African Americans and other minority youth.

A recent HBO special produced a production on violence in America, and observed that by the time a person reaches 18 years of age, he or she has witnessed 18,000 acts of violence on television. Our society is now reaping the harvest of this reality. Stop the Madness seeks to help reverse the effects of this bitter harvest by a combination of initiatives which work together to provide hope and understanding for our youth and our society.

The programs of Stop the Madness are built around three pillars. Those three pillars are education, the other one is recreation, and interpersonal skills. I, as a pastor, feel that we should not leave out value and spirituality because if we want to change people then we need to change their hearts and their mind. So the spirituality plays a very big part in that.

We have created three ares of education, recreation and interpersonal relationships. Among those areas we provide different avenues of reaching and fulfilling those goals.

At the present time, I have been involved over the past 5 years in funeralizing 26 young people, all under the age of 19. To observe this tragedy as it affects our community and affects the family, dealing not only with those who we lose, but also families of those who have the loss, has taken a tremendous toll on their lives.

But nothing to the effect of what happened in 1993. On October 27, 1993, I was teaching a Bible class at our church. There was a call that came on the phone. One of our young ladies got up and answered the phone. She hung the phone up with a stunned look on her face. I said, "Who was it," and she said, "I wish they'd stop playing on the telephone." I asked her, "What did they say?" She said, "They said that your son, T.J., has just been shot in the head."

I stood there stunned because I, like her, was hoping that they were playing on the telephone. But then she said something that made me realize that there was no joke. She said, "I heard your daughter, DeJuan, screaming T.J., T.J., in the background." DeJuan happened to be my 12-year-old daughter. T.J. and DeJuan had gone to a safe haven, the YMCA here in our community, and they were taking piano lessons.

We would always tell them that after piano lessons were over to sit on the couch, by the window, and watch for your mother to pick you up. T.J. was sitting on that same couch that we had told him to sit on, sitting looking out the same window that we had told him to watch for his mother. On the outside an altercation took place, bullets started flying. Two bullets entered the YMCA and one of them lodged in his head.

At that time, when we ran around to the YMCA, I ran through—the police came, and there lay my own 15-year-old son. For the first time in my life, I did not know how to pray. I knew T.J. was a very active young man. I had buried kids that had been shot in the back, in the neck, in the side and in the head, but for certain everyone that had been shot in the head, we ended up funeralizing them.

This community came together and they prayed for my son. After arriving at the emergency room, I watched jagged lines on the monitor begin to get straight. I know it was a supernatural occurrence that took place because when this community began to pray, the straight line began to get jagged again. I'm very proud to say, I thank God and this community for praying for him because I am now proud to say that my 15-year-old son who was shot in the head in 1993, who still carries a bullet lodged in his head, is now my 17-year-old son who recently graduated from Snyder High School and is a prospective student at Ball State in the fall of this year. I'm proud to have him with me this day.

If the question came, does this put a damper on your Stop the Madness efforts? My statement to this community in 1993, was no, this does not put a damper. As a matter of fact, this helps to recommit ourselves to continue to educate our kids, educating our youth about the violence that is in this community.

In a statement in reference to drugs, I would like to make a statement to this panel and that is that I am convinced, I am convinced that if we're really going to wage a war on drugs, we need to start where it begins. I am concerned about all of our young people who, for small offenses are destroying their lives by not only a police record, ended up filling up our jails, but no kids I know have a plane to fly drugs into this community. No kid that I know has a boat to drive drugs across the ocean in a boat. No kid that I know owns a gun factory and no kid that I know makes movies that perpetuate the violence that we're seeing in our world.

I think that if we're going to make a difference, we've got to start where it starts. I believe that we, as a community, have to stop the big drug dealers. If we would stop the drug dealers at the border then we can save a whole lot of kids' lives and we could, as a community, release those that are filling up the jail and give them opportunities like preventative measure to make a difference in their lives.

We have a little short video that we would like to share of the actual shooting of T.J. that we're now using to get the message of Stop the Madness out into this community. We'd also like to say that it is presently being shown in Cleveland, OH, and Chattanooga, TN, and it is at the movie theaters here in Fort Wayne.

[Video shown]

[The prepared statement of Rev. Jordan follows:]

January 1992 presented me with the tragic and unfortunate task of funeralizing a 15 year old young lady who had been shot in the head. It was reported that her death was due to participation in Russian Roulette. At her funeral there were 16 or 17 hundred young people sitting there with disbelief on their faces. Not only did their faces display disbelief, but posed the question: "Who will be next?" It didn't take very long to supply them with the answer. Three weeks later another fifteen year old was shot. This time a young man. Once again Russian Roulette had claimed a young life. I again had to funeralized one of our youth. During the year of 1992 we funeralized 12 young people all under the age of nineteen. In the last five years I have personally funeralized 26 young people due to acts of violence.

After the funerals of the first two 15 years olds. Members of Greater Progressive decided to unite and bring together parents, teachers, city officials and young people. This gathering was to include some young people who were involved in negative behavior. Some labeled these kids gangs. On February 29,1992, 850 people gathered at the Greater Progressive Baptist Church to discuss youth and violence. This coming together was such an overwhelming success that it was decided to proceed with additional programs aimed at alerting the community -at-large about the danger of our youth and their involvement in drugs and violence.

During the summer of 1992, Stop the Madness worked with 216 young people between the ages of 7 to 14 providing a summer camp experience. The camp's focus centered around self-esteem, motivation, and decision-making. Stop the Madness expanded to include a tutorial program during the school year to meet the educational needs of young people with the hope that children would be empowered in their educational setting. Mentors were provided to youth to help them utilize the information they were acquiring. It was hoped that mentors would also provide new and enlightening experiences. Stop The Madness had taken shape and was impacting the lives of our youth and the community.

Mission Statement

Stop the Madness exists for the purpose of advancing creative solutions for ending the needless violence which has come to characterize so much of American life and interpersonal interactions, especially among African-American and other minority youth.

The Need

A recent HBO special production on violence in America has observed that by the time a person reaches eighteen years of age, he/she has witnessed 18,000 acts of violence on television. Our society is now reaping the harvest of this reality. Stop the Madness seeks to help reverse the effects of this bitter harvest by a combination of initiatives which work together to provide hope and understanding for our youth and society.

The programs of Stop the Madness are built around three pillars. These pillars are

Education, Recreation and Interpersonal Relationships. Stop the Madness believes that only as we educate our young people and society about the causes of violence, provide alternatives to violent anti-social behavior and work to understand one another better, can we hope to stem the tide of the violence that has made itself a part of our daily lives.

Starting June 25,1996 Stop The Madness will initiate a new summer program entitled Brother -to-Brother and Sister -to-Sister. These programs are designed to connect older Christians with young people. These programs will meet twice weekly. The young people involved will participate in an hour of instruction and two hours of recreational activities. The curriculum will consist of : Black History which will teach participants about their culture. Learning about one's culture helps to provide a sense of pride and direction. If you don't know where you have been, then you don't know where you are going. Other components of instruction will deal with values, morals and spirituality. I am totally convinced that the only way to help our youth is to change their hearts. Spirituality is very much a part of the African -American tradition and a very strong component in changing lives. Other issues such as; self-esteem, motivation, self-awareness and peer pressure are Issues relevant to the lives of today's youth. Reggie White, the All Pro Defensive Lineman of the Green Bay Packers will share with the participants on the topic "Being the Best You Can Be." A trip to Chicago will climax the summer activities.

Future Plans

Program Components

Education	**Recreational**	**Inter-Personal Relationships**
Video Production	Shepherds	Reconciliation Workshops
Values Clarification Small Groups	Recreational	Jordan's Shepherds of Peace
Newsletters, books	Outreach	Conflict Resolution/Mediation
900 call-in line	Initiatives	

On October 27,1993 the violence that I had diligently fought against became a personal tragedy. While teaching a Bible class the telephone rung and a young lady answered it. She hung up with a stunned look on her face. "I asked her who was it?" and she responded, "I wish they would stop playing on the phone." I then asked, " what did they say?" She replied, " they said your son TJ has just been shot in the head." As I stood likewise hoping someone was playing on the phone she then replied, "I heard your daughter, DeJuan screaming in the background. I immediately ran out of the church, jumped into my car and headed toward the YMCA where both of my children were taking piano lessons. When I arrived, there were police cars, fire trucks, ambulances and people standing all around. As I ran into the building there laying in the floor was my own fifteen year old son bleeding profusely with a bullet wound to his head. I bent down over him and said, "TJ, this is your dad" and as his eyes rolled to the back of his head, I thought I saw him take what was his last breath. I cannot express the emotion that I felt. After burying twelve young people with various gunshot wounds I was certain that this head wound would be a fatal shot to my firstborn son. As I sit here today, I am happy to share that by the grace of God, my fifteen year old son that was wounded that dark fateful night of October is now my 17 year old son who still has a bullet lodged in his head, but two weeks ago graduated from high school and is prospective student at Ball State University. This personal tragedy did nothing more than recommit me to fight against violence particularly among our youth.

God spared my son, but gave me a taste of the hurt and pain that violence inflicts upon families. A pain so devastating that only God can ease. I am convinced that God has placed me in this position to help our young people come to grips with the fact that the decisions they make, for the most part, determine their outcome and be a catalyst to help **Stop the Madness.**

Mr. SOUDER. I know you have to leave at a certain point, so hopefully we'll get back to some questions. You know that I strongly commend you and your efforts in this community. And your son, gave something that I read in the congressional record about 2 weeks ago. One night when we were talking about a number of programs, I was talking about your efforts and the efforts of other pastors in Fort Wayne, the Simba Program, Rev. White's efforts, and Shirley Woods, her Community Center, the Wilson Center. There are a lot of positive things happening and we can easily focus on the negative side.

You've seen firsthand what we hear about, having buried 29 young people, is something that we don't often see and it's important for us to see the emotion that's about that and how you handle that at a personal level, was an example to the city of Fort Wayne, to help unite the city. You are to be commended for it, both you and your son. Andre.

Mr. PATTERSON. First of all, let me thank you for having us. This is Barry Martin, Jr. He's the president of the Simba Club. Simba is a program designed for prevention from Allen Superior Court, Family Relations Division. Basically, we put the program together, Carl Johnson originally put the program together. They hired me to come in to basically run the program, design the program which is designed as it is now.

We're run out of Cooper Teen Center, and basically Simba is a rites of passage group for young men from 8 to 14. But it's a little more than that because we've now taken Simba and designed it into a whole family type of program. We've got involvement with the schools, with the parents, and also now in the community, the young men are now joining the churches, taking classes at the university.

Some of the things that Simba does is just basically curb violence. Like I said, we go to church. It's really difficult for me to explain. We have a creed in which they live up to because you see so much violence, you see so many black youth today disrespecting women, disrespecting their community that when you asked some of the young kids why do they do the things they do, they don't have any answers for you. It's just a part of their environment.

So basically what I do is, we learn with everything we do, through the community. We also go out of the community. As you know, we took them to DC, to visit the White House and do a lot of other things. The one thing that I've found from doing this with these young men, we have 20 young men at this point and all 20 of them are committed. They make the program. They basically, I ask the question you always hear, "Say no to drugs and yes to this and yes to that." Kids need someone to be there. They need to feel a part. They need to come up with the ideas. They need to design their group.

Why are we so effective? One reason we're so effective is because each of them have dedicated themselves to something positive. Right now I have 15 young men, I have 4 that are on the honor roll in school. I have none that's involved in any juvenile activity. This is all for them. They are volunteers. The courts just monitor them as we go through.

Now, you see, I have parents come here who are now involved in their kids' lives as a community. Just last week we had a parent write a play. She's working with the kids and designed a little skit for them. I have fathers who come in and donate their time to cut the youngsters' hair. It's a program that started with kids and now has become a whole family type environment.

I have an informal relationship with parents where we do things as a family. Simba is called a family, with parents, kids and myself. Barry here will say his creed and then we'll talk about the code and ethics in which they live by or which we're trying to get them to live by.

Mr. MARTIN. I am Simba, young, gifted and black. I am a strong black brother, always considerate of my children. I am Simba, young, gifted, and black. I am protector of my community, especially my home and my family. I am Simba, young, gifted and black. I claim responsibilities for my own actions, never blaming others for my decisions. I am Simba, young, gifted and black. I'm a strong young lion, leader of the pack. I am the future.

Mr. PATTERSON. These are the ethics in which we're trying to get to. Simba is very close to me because I grew up in Southeast, DC, so it was programs like this that helped me get to where I am. I had the opportunity to travel the world and play basketball. It's sort of funny how things work out, that you can come back and you can do something like this because a lot of my peers that I grew up back home, and I see them, they always say, "Well, you had a break. You had no way out." There was a young man named Mr. Baxter. He saw me and I was just like these gentlemen, from a dysfunctional family, single parent home and he told me then that was no excuse to grow and do wrong, to get involved in negative things.

I can honestly say I've never had drugs in my body. Hopefully I can say that about these young men. Just because someone cared enough to be there for me. So I'm just doing that now for these gentlemen, giving them the basic values that I had. I don't think you can teach values without virtue and I think young people today need to realize that drugs are going to be there. Violence is going to be there. You need to learn how to act and to respond to these, because as long as you're going to live, there's going to be negative behavior come upon you. It's up to you to deal with it.

That's part of the responsibility. That's it.

[The prepared statement of Mr. Patterson follows:]

Simba

Simba is a prevention program from Allen Superior Court Family Relation Division held at Cooper Teen Center. This program is funded by the Paul Clark Foundation.

Simba is a rites of passage group for boys ages 8 to 14, which is designed to give them the skills to make the transition from boy to manhood smoother and more swiftly. The group now has close to 20 members, with the primary focuses being community service projects, fund raising, Saturday school, and mentorship programs with volunteers throughout the city.

With such negative activities as gangs, drugs, and other destructive behaviors, these boys have dedicated themselves to improving their minds, their bodies, and their spirits. They hold each other accountable for their actions as it affects the group, their family, and their community.

Mr. SOUDER. Thank you. We'll come back to you in a minute. Thank you, Barry, for your presentation. Joe Mann.

Mr. MANN. Congressman Souder, Congressman Hastert, I just want to thank you for inviting us to come and to share from our perspective, from Abundant Life Ministries' angle as what we're doing in this community. I want to commend all of the organizations that are represented here, as well as the many others that are not represented here.

One of our main focuses as an organization, working with the criminal justice system is to network with many of these agencies in order to provide a more complete service. We work right now with prisoners, ex-prisoners, families, individuals with life-controlling problems. We work within the Criminal Justice system here. Primarily, in the Allen County Jail we have four men and women who work in the jail providing services to the entire inmate population. It varies anywhere from 500 to 620 inmates on a given day.

There was recently a lengthy article in the newspaper that talked about jail population. Our chaplains that are there, we have two chaplains, they serve the inmates that are there. We do crises counseling. We do five chapel services a week. We oversee a GED program. That is overseen through our office. We oversee pastoral visitation with any pastoring or religious clergy that would like to come in and visit an inmate. We make sure that they're screened, that they're processed.

On any given week, we will work with up to one-half of the jail population through any one of our services, so it can be anywhere from 200 to 300 and some inmates. The primary focus, within our jail outreach is the substance abuse program. We have, on 90 day cycles, we service 20 men and 20 women who will go through intensive classes in the jail.

I guess I could go back about 4 or 5 years ago, as I began to get more involved with some of the issues within the jail and began to see the real need, as they mentioned in the prior counsel, prior men that were up here, they talked about 75 to 80 percent of the people who were incarcerated, they were all incarcerated for substance abuse problems. So I went to some of the places, Chicago, Detroit, and observed their substance abuse programs. There was no local funding. So we took it upon ourselves to try to receive the funding through our community, through churches, through individuals and businesses so we could fund a substance abuse program within the jail.

I'm happy to say that's been up and running now for 2 years. We've served over 200-some men and women. The materials we use are all basically the 12 step, Bible-based materials. Part of our program is to then have these people processed back into the community and to enact in the program. The aftercare program has a network base all of its own, largely volunteer run. The volunteer base basically oversees Bible studies, support groups, one-on-one, visitation. We try to set up a sponsorship, a mentor program to help acclimate these people back into a positive network.

The real goal is to see these people process back into a care giving congregation where they can establish a new support group. Another main area of focus in the criminal justice system is the Youth Corrections Program, where we have two staff that currently oversee a probation referral program. We oversee in court, volunteers go into the two boys' schools which are DOC operated. And then we have the oversight into some of the training that goes on in the Wood Youth Center in conjunction with Taylor University. So our chaplains oversee that.

We have an aftercare network that's being established, it's somewhat established so far for the youthful offenders who have been incarcerated for a period of time. And then we try to build a network there and that's when youthful offenders go there. It's more of volunteer supporters to work within that area.

We also have a residential program as part of our program that's been established for the last 20 years. As a part of the merger that the residential program used to be called the New Life Christian Center. It is now taking up residence in what used to be the Crow Haven Nursing Home. We are able to serve now 30 men. When we first started we were at a capacity of 8 to 10 men. As recently as last October, we moved our capacity up to 30 men. Right now we're about 27 men at this time. We receive people who are sentenced to us through the criminal justice system. Then we have a gentleman who was in a life sentence. He was on death row for a period of time. He is now being released, the procedure is, he's been incarcerated for 22 years, and placed into our program.

We receive a lot of alternative sentencing individuals who are in for primarily substance abuse. In fact, all of the people up to this point who have came into our program are substance abuse related. We have three phases in our program. The three phases are, the first part is 24 hours a day, 7 days a week, we take home monitoring provision away from that part of the Criminal Justice system. Then we process through their eligibility to get a job after 4 months. We try to teach. The whole premise is getting a whole new foundation for many of the men who come to us as a chronic lifestyle substance abuser.

At that point, I want to just allow my two friends just to briefly share with you what they have gone through and what is going on now.

[The prepared statement of Mr. Mann follows:]

Field Hearing:
Abundant Life Ministries Report:
June 24, 1996

Abundant Life Ministries works with prisoners, ex-prisoners, those with life-controlling problems and their families, in a correctional, residential and aftercare environment. ALM has been in existence since April 1994 and represents the merged ministries of the Allen County Jail Ministry and the New Life Christian Center which both were established in the early 70's.

Corrections:

ALM has four staff ministering in the Allen County Jail. Two work as chaplains and two specialize in the area of substance abuse counseling. The goal is to work with the incarcerated, their families, victims of crime, as well as the corrections staff.

The chaplaincy program serves the entire jail population which will range from 550 - 650 inmates at any given time. Our chaplains work as crisis counselors, facilitate pastoral visits from the community, coordinate 5 chapel services weekly, coordinate the GED program and all library materials distributed to the jail population. On any given week approximately one-half the jail population will attend chapel services.

The substance abuse treatment program works with a select group of 20 men and 20 women in the jail. We host six support groups per week three with the men and three with the women. The curriculum is an open 90 day cycle, there are clinical, educational and spiritual components to the program. The materials we use are through RAPHA and Minerith / Myer resources. The programming is Biblically 12 step based and focuses on substance abuse, stress management, sexual abuse issues. Since it's inception two years ago over 300 men and women have gone through the substance abuse program at the jail.

Locally 75% of all those who are arrested are arrested on drug and alcohol related charges. They were either high when they committed their crime, or they committed their crime to get resources to get high.

Youth Corrections program:

The ALM youth corrections ministry has chaplaincy outreach into the Indiana boys school, trains volunteers to work within Wood Youth Center, provides probation referral services to youthful offenders on probation and aftercare services to those who have come through the youth correctional system.

Men's Residential Program:

Currently ALM serves up to 30 men in our residential program. Our residential program over the last year has been modeled after a national program called Teen Challenge. We have had over 105 men enter the program since May 1994.

We average 1 out of 10 who enter graduate the one year program, so far we have a 100% success rate with our graduates. Teen Challenge who has been in existence for over 25 years has a 80% success rate for all those who graduate. It is projected that we will have seven to nine men graduate this year. Success rate being they do not recidivate nor go back to their old life style of substance abuse. We project that by the end of 1996 we will have a 1 out of 8 ratio for those who enter our program and then complete the entire year.

Our one-year program consists of three phases each lasting four months. The progression of phases provide a range from intense supervision to limited accountability and oversight. The first phase provides 24 hour, 7 day a week supervision, during the second phase our students are eligible to go to work in the community receiving more freedoms and more responsibilities. Third phase students are given almost complete freedom to come and go as we provide accountability thus enabling the students to develop habits of positive choices.

All of our programming is Bible based covering topics such as: anger management, substance abuse issues, relationships, parenting, social-skills, life-skills, other classes on the Bible.

One-half of our clients are sentenced through the criminal justice system, the others are walk-in who also, for the most part have had some prior involvement with the criminal justice system. At this point all of our clients have had problems with substance abuse issues.

Aftercare:
This area of outreach works with ex-prisoners, graduates of our residential program, and their families. This area of ministry started in April 1995. Through a large volunteer network we "track" 50 to 80 individuals at a time. The goal is to see these people established in a care giving church congregation, a community of people who will provide a new support base and structure.

The Aftercare services provided are: Weekly small group Bible studies, substance abuse support groups, one-on-one home visits, referral services to help with jobs and other practical needs.

Executive Directors Personal Experience:
I have been incarcerated for 22 months for substance abuse issues which lead to other criminal activity. While incarcerated I became a Christian and was paroled in 1983 to a program like ALM located in Lindale, Texas. It is my first hand experience programs like ALM work and the difference is in the Christ-centered biblical program.

Brief words from:
Mike Douglas & Vaughn McAfee: both of these men have been incarcerated a number of times, have been severely addicted to drugs and are currently in phase three of our residential program. They will each share briefly a small portion of their past and the impact the ALM program has had on their lives.

Joe Mann is currently the Executive Director of Abundant Life Ministries

Abundant Life Ministries works with prisoners, ex-prisoners, those with life-controlling problems and their families - in a correctional, residential, and aftercare environment.

Joe holds a Bachelors degree in Bible and Theology. He has been in social ministry for over ten years and has been ordained for eight years through Broadway Christian Church in Fort Wayne. Through Broadway Christian Church he and his wife Marilyn spent two and one-half years in Asia, living in Hong Kong, Taiwan and Singapore involved in social outreach.

Joe currently is a Sheriffs Department Chaplain, he serves on the Fort Wayne Community Corrections Board of Directors. He is actively involved leadership of a weekly Bible study with Broadway Christian Church.

In 1981 Joe was incarcerated for 22 months in California for reasons related to substance abuse and burglary. While Joe was incarcerated he became a Christian and attributes the change in his life to the power of God and the application of Biblical principles. When Joe was released from prison he went to a transitional ministry in Texas similar to Abundant Life Ministries. There he received training and direction to pursue full-time ministry.

Joe grew up in central California. He enjoys outdoor activities, most sports, reading, and taking long walks with his wife. Joe and his wife Marilyn have been married for over 11 years and currently reside in the south side of Fort Wayne.

Mr. DOUGLAS. It's an honor to be here. I'm a redeemed drug addict and alcoholic. I abused drugs and alcohol for 25 years. I've been incarcerated in prisons and jails for at least 12 years of my life. My addiction started at a very young age of about 13. I was a heroin addict and I also distributed drugs to support my habit. At the age of 17, I was headed for prison and I stayed incarcerated until I was 28 years old. When I got out of prison, my addiction continued.

I would like to add also that in the prison system, I could carry on my addiction. There was enough drugs available in prison to allow me to be a heroin addict in there also. When I did get out, I continued my addiction by the use of alcohol. It ruined my life. I was married, had children. I lost everything I had through that addiction to alcohol and drugs. It was an overdose of drugs that brought me to Abundant Life Ministries.

It was through Abundant Life Ministries that I got a relationship with Jesus Christ. From that moment that I accepted Christ into my life, my life changed. It's been about a year and a half now I've been serving the Lord. The Lord does do miracles. A year and a half ago I was an addict, alcoholic, a thief, ex-convict. Today, I am counselling kids at a youth camp, inner-city kids, and that's what I'm doing all summer is counselling them and teaching them about Christ.

Mr. MACILFEY. Thank you, Congressman Souder, Congressman Hastert. This truly is a privilege to sit here before you and speak. I, too, up until 9 months ago was a slave to heroin/cocaine for over 25 years of my life. I'm presently 42 years old, and up until that point and time, 9 months ago when I hit the doors of Abundant Life Ministries, I had been in and out of prisons, in and out of jails, I've been to Richmond State Hospital drug addictions twice, I've been to over a dozen drug treatments here, including Washington House. I didn't care about anything. My life was a total mess.

Throughout all this time, God had a plan for Vaughn and the plan was for me to enter those doors of Abundant Life Ministries one day and get my life back on track. Through that program at Abundant Life Ministries, I have been nourished back through people like Joe Mann and the administrators and the people that are there, they have helped nourish me back through God's will. It can only come from God and his people that nursed me back.

My spiritual needs were a wreck and I needed that spiritual healing. Today, I can honestly say that I'm a counselor at Still Water Ministries and a chaplain also for the youth. Like I said, God brought me to this place and I just give him the praise, the Lord, that he so much deserves. I want to thank you all for allowing me the time to share this with you.

Mr. SOUDER. Thank you very much for sharing that, coming forward and sharing that. Mr. Davenport, I know you have done many years of giving over at Washington House, of yourself, and many different areas, and we appreciate your coming.

Mr. DAVENPORT. First of all, I'd like to thank Congressman Souder and Congressman Hastert for inviting me. Next time, I'd like you to let me hear all the other testimonies, then I'll write mine because I hear a lot of things that bring on a little light to me, things that have happened in the community.

Washington House has been in this community for 23 years. We started on Fulton as a bunch of drunks trying to take care of a bunch of other drunks. We proceeded on to where we're at today. We have a building on Catalpa Street. We do three kinds of treatment there. We have residential treatment, detox and outpatient. A lot of things like Rev. Jordan was talking about, about the funerals that he's attended. I see a lot of young people sick. Beautiful young girls that look like old women. Men that can't stand up, can't do anything, they're just vegetables because of the substance abuse.

Personally, at the Washington House, I don't see it getting any better. I heard the first panel talking about the war on drugs, that's a poor name for it, I think. But I don't think we're gaining. Before I came here today I talked to some of our clients and I asked out clients about what's going on in the street. What they tell me is that there's just as much on the streets today, it's weaker than it was before. I'm talking about cocaine. The cocaine is weaker, but there's still plenty of it on the streets. You could go to almost any street corner and get it in any part of the city or county, and the outlying areas.

Indiana just came up with a, it's not new, it's all over the United States now, managed care for substance abusers. It really set the treatment community back. Washington House itself will lose $700,000 in State grants because of this treatment. We feel like that the biggest thing it's going to hurt is residential treatment, places where people who have tried to get off of the substance, can't do it with outpatient and other things need that residential treatment. And we see that decreasing greatly. In order to counter these things, we've had to go out in the community and do things we've never had to do before.

We've always been a third-party pay and never really worried about anybody having money or not. To come to the Washington House, it was always a place where anybody could go regardless of their status. We've done a lot of things. We went to a court system in Ohio. What we did, Judge Campbell in VanWert, OH, real heavy on penalties for people doing that, but he's also into treatment. What he will do is he will put somebody in his jail and he will leave them in there a week to 10 days just to let them see what the jail is like. If they so desire, he will take them out of there and put them in treatment.

After they leave treatment, he will look at the recommendations of the treatment center to decide what he will do next. He puts them back in jail for a while, a few days just to let them know that he's still there, still around. He will try to put them in a halfway house, like Abundant Life, somewhere where he can take these people and make good citizens out of them.

That's been a real successful program in VanWert. They have talked to Wapokoneta, OH, and they want to do the same thing in Wapokoneta. We've been unsuccessful doing it here in the city of Fort Wayne, but we're still working on it.

Another program that we have, that I believe came from your office, we talked about—we sat down with General Motors and General Motors is the type of place that they want to keep people on the job, as many as they can. So they came up with a program, it's called the Work Host Program. We've also talked to Dana about this program. What that program is, this individual goes to work every day. We take them to work. We pick them up at work. They come back to the treatment center and they do 4 hours of treatment in the center and stay there, just like residential treatment. In order for us to get to that level, what we did, we took day treatment, if you're familiar with any insurance language, they got a day treatment that somebody just comes in the day time and then they go home at night.

That's a much lower rate than residential treatment. The insurance companies agreed that they would extend the amount of days of treatment under day treatment and we would keep them for 24 hours and do all the things that I told you we do. Average stay is around 40 days. We treated eight people so far in this program and seven of the eight are back at General Motors and not using today. It's been very successful. It's a good program.

Most of the people, after they got out of there, we put in a halfway house. One good thing has came from the new State program is that we're interacting with other agencies. Right now, the people that we're going to serve under the new program which starts July 1st, next week, we have got contracts with people that we will do probably mostly detox for them. The way the program works is the State provides $2,700 per client, per year. This client has to have 1 year's treatment. Whoever the provider is has to see to it that this person gets all the help they can for a full year.

So they will find these things out, like detox, residential, inpatient, whatever they need to try to get this person off the substance. They get their money up front and they pay for all of the treatment. If they use up their $27, $2,800, the treatment is on them. So we've had to do some things there.

So we've done a lot of innovative things to help keep the Washington House open and a good source for the community. We couldn't do it without the help of most of the people at this table because we interact a lot. Abundant Life, quite a bit, one of their pastors George MacGowen, is on our Board of Directors. We have other people on our Board of Directors that sit on some these other agencies so we can interact with their agency.

But it's an overall effort to try to make things happen. You requested some demographics and I put a copy of the demographics on my thing, but this is just real quick. I was listening to the first panel and they were talking about substance abuse and legalizing drugs. Alcohol is a legal drug. Last year we treated 1,103 people for alcoholism. We treated 590 people for cocaine, 558 people for marijuana. That's the way it's broke down.

Most of the people that we see are addicted to at least two drugs, one of them being alcohol. Most everyone is addicted to alcohol. So it's a big thing. I can't see by alcohol, which is a legal drug, that many people, how it will help us to ever legalize any of the other drugs. It would be a catastrophe.

With that, I thank you again for having me here. Any further questions you have, I'll be glad to answer for you.

[The prepared statement of Mr. Davenport follows:]

WASHINGTON HOUSE TREATMENT CENTER

2720 CULBERTSON STREET • FORT WAYNE, INDIANA 46802 • FAX 436-7904 • (219) 432-8684

June 24, 1996

Presented by Ron J. Davenport, Operations Director

Washington House Treatment Center, a 501 (3) (C) not for profit, has been servicing the low-income; no-income client for twenty-three (23) years with funding coming from state and federal grants (60%) and donations from the community 40%. **Beginning July 1, we will lose approximately $700,000 in direct funding from state grant due to the state going to managed care for chemical abuse treatment for the poor.** It is our opinion that this program will seriously hurt inpatient treatment as we know it today. Inpatient treatment is necessary for people who have tried other means of treatment and failed (outpatient, detox, self-help programs). If we ever hope to win the war on drugs, some means must be established to treat the addicts and alcoholics who presently are on our streets, in our jails and who are homeless.

We are working with third party payers, court systems and managed care providers in order to continue our services to the community.

One of our new programs we are now using with General Motors is the **Work Host program.** The purpose of the Work Host Program is to provide a safe place for chemically dependent people to live and receive treatment while continuing to work at their places of employment. The program involves two stages: Partial Hospitalization followed by Continuing Care. It is designed for those individuals who have failed to maintain sobriety with previous treatment attempts, i.e. the chronic relapser. Clients will be transported to and from their employment. They will be picked up at the end of their shifts and returned to Washington House Treatment Center for 4 hours of chemical dependency education and therapy. On weekends they will attend and participate in our regular residential treatment programming.

The Work Host program is designed to have a longer length of stay than other treatment options, to allow the relapse-prone individual adequate time to maintain abstinence during the critical period of cravings and to break the cycle of relapse.

The Work Host Program is done at a lower negotiated rate than regular inpatient treatment, thus enabling us to get the extra days of treatment.

An Equal Opportunity/Affirmative Action Agency

Washington House Treatment Center - (219) 432-8684
2720 Culbertson Street, Fort Wayne, IN 46802 FAX: (219) 436-7904

Summary of Comparison of Demographic Data for Six Year Period

Admissions:

Admissions to the detoxification and residential programs during the year 1995 were both slightly higher than the previous year. Admissions to the outpatient programs are roughly twice the previous year, which is to be expected as the previous year (1994) was the first year these programs were functional, and were only conducted for roughly the last six months of that year.

Client Gender

Viewing the entire six year period, the percentages of male and female admissions note an overall increase in the number of female admissions, although the number of such admissions during 1995 are slightly decreased from the previous year.

Client Race

The year 1995 noted a marked decrease in the number of admissions of Black clients. The number of admissions of "Other" races (Hispanic, American Indian, Asian, etc.) was roughly the same as the previous year, resulting in an increase in the percentage of admissions of Caucasian clients.

Income Levels

As noted in the previous reports, the percentage of persons with incomes over $10,000 has shown a steady increase.

Type of Abuser

Compared to the previous years, the percentages of admissions who are using a single non-alcohol drug has increased substantially over the six year period. The percentage of admissions who are using only alcohol has reversed a trend of decrease and increased slightly this year. There has been a corresponding decrease in the number of admissions who are poly-drug users this year.

Age Groups

During the year 1993, the Board of Directors elected to modify the detoxification admission criteria to admit persons over the age eighteen only. With the exception of admissions made up of the 19-20 year old age group which increased slightly in terms of persons, the trend this year has been towards an older clientele, with admissions from the 31-40 year old group making up nearly half of all admissions. Admissions aged 31 and older made up roughly two-thirds of all admissions this year.

Current Substances of Abuse

The most notable changes in this area are increases in the percentages of admissions using marijuana, heroin and other opiates. Slightly less than half of all admissions were currently using cocaine, which has shown a decreasing trend since a peak in 1993. The use of alcohol has increased this year, and was indicated by about 85% of all admissions.

County of Residence

This information is provided to note the areas where our clients reside. This information is based on Fiscal Year admissions. There is also a cumulative collection of all admissions from FY 88 through FY 95, with the exception of detoxification statistics for FY 88, which are not available.

Mr. SOUDER. Thank you. Without objection, we'll put all your testimony into the record. I wondered, Mr. Mann, would you be willing to share some of your background, too? You personally have gone through some of this in addition to your ministry——

Mr. MANN. I became a Christian while I was incarcerated, 14 years ago. As you know, in northern California, I had a history since I was 12 years old, involved in substance abuse which led to all different kinds of juvenile delinquency and criminal behavior. I got involved in burglaries and different types of robberies. At 18 I was arrested. In the first year I was arrested six times. During the final arrest I was considering suicide. While I was in this place, I started reading some materials through the jail ministry there and it talked about Jesus Christ coming and changing my life. I got on my knees there in jail and prayed, "God, Jesus Christ, if you prove it all, I'll follow you forever." There were some people that came into jail and talked to me about God and I still wasn't convinced.

I thought Christianity was just for little old ladies or whatever. I was convinced over a short period of time. I was paroled and released after 22 months of incarceration, to a place much like Abundant Life Ministry. That place, its focus wasn't just getting people off drugs. Its goal was to prepare people for the ministry, to prepare people for life in general. So we've taken some of that same philosophy and implemented it into our program at Abundant Life.

So it's not just to get a guy off of drugs, it's to prepare Vaughn and Mike here so they can go back and give back to the community the part of the program and the strong words of God.

Mr. SOUDER. Out of the power of your words and the words of Michael and Vaughn, you've lived through it. Part of the power of Andre's words are, you've been in the communities and you've made it through and didn't fall. Part of the power of you as a pastor is you've buried young people and you've gone through it in your own family. I commend you for standing forth and reaching out to others. I mean, I grew up in a very protected background and I sit there and preach it and everybody says, "Yeah, easy for him to talk." But it's not easy for all of you to talk. You're all to be commended for doing that. One of the other things is, do you take Government money? Would you want Government money and have you been through this experience?

Mr. MANN. Well, we would take it if we were still able to proclaim the same Biblical message as we're claiming today. I understand that there are some restrictions, and so we pursue private sector funding, businesses, churches, and individuals. But I know that there is much conversation in regard to various types of tax benefits.

Mr. SOUDER. Have you talked with any agencies? Have they suggested to you that there would be a problem with your approach?

Mr. MANN. No. No. Not private funding—as long as there would be no limitation. I've talked to various people and they've said, you know, "Would you consider changing your message in order to get more funding?" I said, "No. I would rather work out of a trailer and do what we do now. It's the message of Jesus Christ. That makes the difference."

Mr. SOUDER. Have you ever talked to a Government agency about the grants?

Mr. MANN. No.

Mr. SOUDER. I realize that they have a different mission statement because the danger is if you got involved initially, the question is down the road what do you have, because you do believe that the spiritual component is critical. You also, Rev. Jordan, alluded to the spirituality and the need to change people's hearts. Could you talk about how that's effecting youth today and how do we reach out to the young people? I know we have the youth ensemble that T.J. is in, and what else? How do we deal with that today, with MTV, with movies, with lack of job opportunities?

Rev. JORDAN. Kids are filling their voids with something and if they're not given positive things, things of value, things with morals, then they fill it with junk. Seven years ago when I came to Fort Wayne, I had a large church with no members. When I began to work with young people, people began to tell me that young people were not interested in church. But I beg to differ with them. We stuck and we stayed and now we're sitting chairs in the isles on Sunday mornings. Since January 1, we've taken in over 400 young people to our church this year.

You were there the other month, you saw all the young people that were in the church. Young people are looking for something. I think basically what we have done by taking value, morals, spirituality, out of the schools and out of other places, we've created this monster that we're trying to correct today. So the real issue is we need to get back to the basics and if we got back to the basics and started filling peoples' lives with positive and God then we can move on, we could clean some of the beds up at the Washington House. We could give Joe more room and I could stop doing so many funerals. That would be the way to go.

Mr. SOUDER. T.J., I'm sure you've seen many kids you've grown up with struggle with the different things. Could you just share for the record and for us how you've seen, maybe without saying names or anything, some people that you know in school who may have gotten involved and started carrying a gun, gotten involved with drugs? What would lead one person next to you to have this kind of spin out, where he had—spirituality is a part of it. Could you give us a little bit of a feeling for what you've seen personally with other people around you in school and other places?

Master JORDAN. Well, in that situation, I would have to say that their surroundings and their environment, people that they see everyday, things that they hear, people that they hang with would cause them to do something like that. The music that they listen to. Some people, when listening to music, it seems like when, like a computer. You put something into a computer, you get that same information out. You put something bad in your mind, you get the same thing out. Some people, when they listen to music like that or watch television shows like that, they don't know how to overlook all of that. Such as younger kids, when they look at somebody, somebody that they admire, that they would like to be like, they try to portray themselves to be like that.

I think that the surroundings and the environment that people are in will cause them to take action like that.

Mr. SOUDER. I wanted to come back when we were getting the testimony, the man from the Indiana State Police, he had a long testimony and he was trying to edit as he was talking. This is one of the things that he took out. Recently we were able to monitor the price of LSD in Indiana. Before the rock group "Grateful Dead," came to Indiana, a hit would average about $5. After the "Dead" arrived in town, that same dose would only cost $1 because the market was saturated. There are people who follow tours from city to city and have their suppliers Fed-Ex them packages full of LSD. That is an exact example of the inter-relationship of the, we had so much LSD coming in that it drove the price down 40 percent of what it was when the "Grateful Dead" would show up at a concert. We have kids that say, "Oh, it's meaningless." But it does have some impact. Garbage in, garbage out is what my mom always taught me. Andre, maybe you can, I know you've given us some impact. One of the things that always, I know you've got the anti-gang t-shirts and the drugs and you've got your kids out there selling different things. One thing that always strikes me and Barry is a good example of that, is that they all look so cheerful and hopeful. That's going to be the real challenge to go up the next steps.

If you manage to succeed with someone, people say it's impossible, you did. You obviously had a basketball talent. But part of our job is to try to figure out how to get opportunity in other areas, other than just sports and look forward to working with you. Maybe you can give us some insight as to some of the things that kids that get to the junior high level, 14, 15-year-olds, and particularly there are still drug problems in all parts of the community, particularly young, black African-Americans who have this tremendous hope in elementary school and just kind of see this burn out in junior high and high school. How do we try to transition that gap?

Mr. PATTERSON. Basically, what I do is I take the young man and we talk about everything. We talk about sex, drugs, how it affects you. Some of what we do is just make everything fun. Make the kids grow into it and teach them while they're having fun. A lot of times, you'll find out that kids will come up and they know more about things than you do. So what we do, or what I do is basically I take them, we go out into the community, we let them see the next phase. Whatever the first phase is, you know there's a next phase.

If you start hanging with someone that you know has a relationship to a gang, well you automatically know that he's just not hanging out with you to be your friend. There's another phase to it. He's trying to pull you in. He wants to suck you into his world. You have to be aware that if someone offered you a sip of alcohol, then you know there's a next phase because once you get a taste that gives you a craving. You want more. So, basically we talk about all of these things and how to combat them and how to walk away from them.

They have enough self-esteem so that they know that not being a part of any crowd doesn't mean that you're not cool. Basically that's it. Just simple——

Mr. SOUDER. For the record, I want to insert, it may take us, if there's no objection, it may take us a day or two to sort this out. But there's a new survey released today by Bill Bailey at Indiana

University and one of the things that, let's see if I can find the number here real quick, 7 percent of Hoosier students reported some use of alcohol prior to age 7. More than 12 percent use alcohol by age 9. Four percent of Hoosier children has reported experimenting with cigarettes by age 7, 9 percent by age 9. Grades, we had a higher than normal than national use on drugs.

So the highest risk population is already in trouble by age 7 and 9. That's an extraordinary figure. I'd like to ask more questions of all of you, but I will yield to Congressman Hastert.

Mr. HASTERT. Thank you, Mr. Souder. It's incredible the line-up that we have here, and the stories certainly tell what a community can do. I've been an advocate for a long time, we knew we did have to start to win the war on drugs, to stop this stuff from Mexico, Peru to Bolivia to Colombia. We know that we have to work together. The first step is to keep it outside of our borders.

You're right, if we could start to—it's not too late for those that have already been incarcerated who certainly don't have to bow nose, who are yet to be born, yet to develop. The more we can keep off our streets, the more young men and young women that we free from this menace. It's also two sides, you have the supply side and you also have the demand side. I've been in Congress for a while and it's always been my promise that the demand side is not just the laws that you pass.

We could talk the law, put more people in prison, you could put more money on top of more money, some of it's effective and some of it's not. It has to be our churches and it has to be our schools and it has to be our parents and the elders in the community all of a sudden don't shake their head and say, "Well, there's nothing we can do about it. We'll just turn our head, look the other way." It has to be the people like yourselves to get the community involved, to get the kids involved and get people involved. That's the way to stop it.

I just want to commend you. We could go on and ask questions all night long. I've learned a lot of things from you and I think it's been extraordinary testimony here before this panel. I just want to take my hats off to all of you for the good job that you've done. You're right. We need to look for other places other than just temporal places here on earth and I meant that's how we really need to turn this thing around. Thank you, very much and I give back my time.

Mr. SOUDER. Thank you. I also want to look for the exact copy, I'd like to hold the record open for a few days and——

Mr. HASTERT. Absolutely no objection.

Mr. SOUDER [continuing]. To look for the additional materials, we had an informal hearing out at the old Fort Wayne Y where a number of people gave testimony, various groups and people from Stop the Madness, I want to make sure that somebody can get that. Also, I want to thank Michael and Vaughn, I didn't get to ask you some questions there, but for coming forth and the importance now as you're talking to these young people and standing as a role model, you're the type people who can really make a difference in our community. You've been in the middle of it and young people can look and you can talk first hand and say, "This is what happened to me. Now look what's happened to me." It's tremendous that you're wanting to stand up and wanting to do that. And also Washington House for their long efforts and continuing to work together. I thank you all for coming today, and with this the Subcommittee on National Security, International Affairs, and Criminal Justice meeting is adjourned.

[Whereupon, at 6:15 p.m., the subcommittee was adjourned.]

[Additional information submitted for the hearing record follows:]

ALLEN COUNTY DRUG TASK FORCE

1995 ANNUAL REPORT

PROGRAM GOAL:

The continuing goal of The Allen County Drug Task Force is to enhance, through joint investigation, the ability of local law enforcement agencies to remove specifically targeted criminal persons and/or organizations involved in major distribution, sale, or importation of controlled substances and associated crimes in and around the Fort Wayne, Allen County area, through identification, investigation, arrest, prosecution, seizure and conviction.

GRANT #95-DB-036 OPERATIONS:

In the past year of Task Force operations we have executed fourteen (14) search warrants some of which were used for the purpose of directly gathering intelligence for four (4) major drug cases which the Task Force is currently pursuing. During this pursuit we have arrested some individuals which have become "co-operating individuals" and are assisting us in furthering our investigations. Two (2) of the four (4) cases have led us directly to cocaine and crack suppliers known to us and the Federal authorities in the Detroit, Michigan area. One of the other cases has led us to the State of Texas. Investigators there are now in the process of investigating the shipping of cocaine and marijuana to the northeast part of the country via private vehicles and through the use of the United States Postal Service and other private mail and package carriers.

We were involved in one case that required the service of six (6) search warrants at the same time, on the same day which led to the arrest of five persons in Fort Wayne. Through this case we were successful in the closing of a crack and heroin operation from the South Bend, Indiana area. We confiscated over 361 grams of heroin from one location with a street value of over $184,000.00.

Another case involved the arrest of persons in the Fort Wayne area which directly led to the later arrest of suppliers in Tempe, Arizona. Those arrests then led investigators to the Southern border states and the identification of major narcotic traffickers whose dope was ending up on the streets of Fort Wayne and Allen County. This case is now a high profile Federal case in the state of Texas, Southern Federal District.

Two cases this year with the United States Postal Services involved cooperation between several Federal and Local agencies with the Task Force as we delivered packages and then arrested the subjects that received them. These investigation resulted in the seizure of more than seventy (70) pounds of marijuana, the identification of shippers, receivers and several illegal immigrants.

During the year the Task Force was able to assist several other Law Enforcement Drug Units from within the borders of the State of Indiana. These cases led to the identification of drug suppliers from the Fort Wayne area and resulted in the arrests of persons in the other Units jurisdiction.

As always our investigations are continuing.

METRO INTELLIGENCE UNIT

YEAR END SUMMARY

YEAR 1995

	DAYS I MONTH	MONEY SEIZED	DRUGS/grams					GUNS		ARRESTS				AGE		SEX		RACE			
			Marijuana	Cocaine	Heroin	Hallucin	Other	H	L	MISD	FEL	WAR	MISC	-18	18+	M	F	W	B	H	OTH
SUN	35	$ 0	0.0	0.0	0.0	0.0	0.0	0	0	0	0	0	0	0	0	0	0	0	0	0	0
MON	35	$ 40,599	44.5	104.1	0.3	0.1	0.0	4	3	33	15	13	40	2	47	44	3	6	42	1	0
TUE	35	$ 66	40.7	2.9	0.1	0.0	0.0	1	0	21	7	19	30	5	47	43	9	14	36	2	0
WED	35	$ 101	64.9	11.7	0.0	0.0	0.0	9	0	30	16	15	46	7	55	59	2	5	54	3	0
THU	35	$ 2,109	68.9	9.0	0.0	0.0	0.0	2	7	27	15	16	30	4	37	31	9	3	37	1	0
FRI	35	$ 2,092	87.9	37.5	0.0	0.0	0.0	2	0	53	30	33	56	6	75	77	4	21	55	5	0
SAT	35	$ 739	436.7	30.6	0.0	0.0	0.0	5	1	19	18	21	16	7	22	28	1	6	23	0	0
TOTAL	245	$ 45,706	743.6	195.8	0.4	0.1	0.0	23	11	183	101	117	218	31	283	565	28	55	247	12	0

COMMENTS/OTHER INFO:

OVER 45,000.00 DOLLARS SEIZED

101- FELONY ARRESTS

34- GUNS CONFISCATED

743.6 GRAMS OF MARIJUANA SEIZED

195.8 GRAMS OF COCAINE SEIZED

117 WARRANTS SERVED

183 MISDEMEANOR ARRESTS

619 TOTAL ARREST,S MADE BY THE FT.WAYNE/ALLEN CO. METRO UNIT FOR APPROX. 6 MONTHS

METRO INTELLIGENCE UNIT

MONTHLY SUMMARY

MONTH JANUARY YEAR 1996

	DAYS IN MONTH	MONEY SEIZED	DRUGS/grams					GUNS		ARRESTS			WARRANTS		AGE		SEX		RACE			
			Marijuana	Cocaine	Heroin	Hallucin	Other	H	L	FEL	MISD	MISC	FEL	OTH	-18	18+	M	F	W	B	H	OTH
SUN	4	$ 0	0.0	0.0	0.0	0.0	0.0	0	0	0	0	0	0	0	0	0	0	0	0	0	0	0
MON	5	$ 345	29.0	12.0	0.0	0.0	0.0	0	0	8	11	8	0	9	1	9	11	1	3	9	0	0
TUE	5	$ 0	6.5	1.1	0.1	0.0	0.0	0	0	5	2	3	0	2	1	6	5	2	2	5	0	0
WED	5	$ 0	7.0	0.3	0.0	0.0	0.0	0	0	3	9	15	2	10	0	18	12	6	3	15	0	0
THU	4	$ 0	0.8	2.5	0.0	0.0	0.0	0	0	2	10	16	0	9	2	21	23	1	4	18	1	0
FRI	4	$ 1,836	0.0	0.0	0.0	0.0	0.0	0	0	0	5	8	2	5	4	10	12	2	2	12	0	0
SAT	4	$ 0	0.0	0.0	0.0	0.0	0.0	0	0	0	0	0	0	0	0	0	0	0	0	0	0	0
TOTAL	31	$ 2,181	43.3	15.9	0.1	0.0	0.0	0	0	18	37	50	4	35	8	64	63	12	14	59	1	0

COMMENTS/OTHER INFO:

METRO INTELLIGENCE UNIT

MONTHLY SUMMARY

MONTH FEBRUARY YEAR 1996

	DAYS IN	MONEY	DRUGS/grams					GUNS		ARRESTS			WARRANT		AGE		SEX		RACE			
	MONTH	SEIZED	Marijuana	Cocaine	Heroin	Hallucin	Other	H	L	FEL	MISD	MISC	FEL	OTH	-18	18+	M	F	W	B	H	OTH
SUN	4	$ 0	0.1	0.0	0.0	0.0	0.0	0	0	0	6	5	0	0	3	0	2	1	3	0	0	0
MON	4	$ 0	0.0	0.0	0.0	0.0	0.0	0	0	3	5	2	0	3	4	2	3	3	3	3	0	0
TUE	4	$ 0	3.5	1.1	0.0	0.0	0.0	0	0	1	1	1	0	0	0	4	4	0	3	1	0	0
WED	4	$ 6,992	2.2	144.9	0.0	0.0	0.0	5	0	6	1	0	0	0	0	3	2	1	1	2	0	0
THU	5	$ 0	440.0	0.4	0.0	0.0	0.0	0	1	4	16	6	5	4	0	13	11	2	7	6	0	0
FRI	5	$ 0	0.0	0.8	0.0	0.0	0.0	0	0	0	3	3	0	0	1	3	4	0	3	1	0	0
SAT	4	$ 0	0.0	0.0	0.0	0.0	0.0	0	0	0	0	0	0	0	0	0	0	0	0	0	0	0
TOTAL	30	$ 6,992	445.8	147.2	0.0	0.0	0.0	5	1	14	32	17	5	7	8	25	26	7	20	13	0	0

COMMENTS/OTHER INFO: RAIDS WERE CONDUCTED AT FOUR LOCATIONS. ONE STOLEN VEHICLE WAS RECOVERED.

MEMBERS ALSO ASSISTED IN APPREHENSION OF THREE ARMED ROBBERY SUSPECTS.

METRO INTELLIGENCE UNIT

MONTHLY SUMMARY

MONTH MARCH YEAR 1996

	DAYS IN	MONEY	DRUGS/grams					GUNS		ARRESTS			WARRANTS		AGE		SEX		RACE			
	MONTH	SEIZED	Marijuana	Cocaine	Heroin	Hallucin	Other	H	L	FEL	MSD	MISC	FEL	OTH	-18	18+	M	F	W	B	H	OTH
SUN	5	$ 0	0.0	0.0	0.0	0.0	0.0	0	0	0	0	0	0	0	0	0	0	0	0	0	0	0
MON	4	$ 0	6.0	0.7	0.7	0.0	0.0	0	0	3	12	19	7	1	4	9	12	1	5	8	0	0
TUE	4	$ 0	0.0	0.0	0.0	0.0	0.0	1	0	1	2	2	0	0	0	3	3	0	2	1	0	0
WED	4	$ 0	0.0	1.5	0.0	0.0	0.0	0	0	2	9	3	0	8	4	6	10	0	1	9	0	0
THU	4	$ 0	5.7	0.0	0.0	0.0	0.0	0	0	1	3	5	1	2	3	6	8	1	3	6	0	0
FRI	5	$ 0	30.5	0.0	0.0	0.0	0.0	1	0	1	12	8	1	14	0	19	16	3	6	9	4	0
SAT	5	$ 0	0.0	0.0	0.0	0.0	0.0	0	0	0	0	0	0	0	0	0	0	0	0	0	0	0
TOTAL	31	$ 0	42.2	2.2	0.7	0.0	0.0	2	0	8	38	37	9	25	11	43	49	5	17	33	4	0

COMMENTS/OTHER INFO:

METRO INTELLIGENCE UNIT

MONTHLY SUMMARY

MONTH APRIL YEAR 1996

	DAYS IN	MONEY	DRUGS/grams					GUNS		ARRESTS			WARRANTS		AGE		SEX		RACE			
	MONTH	SEIZED	Marijuana	Cocaine	Heroin	Hallucin	Other	H	L	FEL	MISD	MISC	FEL	OTH	-18	18+	M	F	W	B	H	OTH
SUN	4	$ 0	0.0	0.0	0.0	0.0	0.0	0	0	0	0	3	0	0	0	3	2	1	1	1	1	0
MON	5	$ 0	0.4	0.0	0.0	0.0	0.0	0	0	0	16	13	4	2	1	22	21	2	4	17	2	0
TUE	5	$ 0	1.5	7.4	0.0	0.0	0.0	0	0	1	6	9	1	2	2	8	8	2	2	8	0	0
WED	4	$ 0	3.9	1.6	0.0	0.0	0.0	0	0	0	9	11	2	6	0	15	12	3	3	10	2	0
THU	4	$ 0	109.8	0.0	0.0	0.0	0.0	0	0	2	4	7	1	3	1	9	8	2	7	2	1	0
FRI	4	$ 0	5.0	0.0	0.0	0.0	0.0	0	0	3	6	4	1	4	2	3	4	1	3	2	0	0
SAT	4	$ 0	0.0	0.0	0.0	0.0	0.0	0	0	0	0	0	0	0	0	0	0	0	0	0	0	0
TOTAL	30	$ 0	120.6	9.0	0.0	0.0	0.0	0	0	6	41	47	9	17	6	60	55	11	20	40	6	0

COMMENTS/OTHER INFO:

Four County Transitional Living, Inc.
227 1/2 West Maumee Street
Angola, IN 4708

(219) 665-7700

1995 Report of Four County Transitional Living

William Kuhn was hired as director of the 4 C.T.L. facility on Feb.1, 1995. He spent the first two months observing existing half-way houses and supervising the completion of our physical plant at 227½ West Maumee St. in Angola, IN. The time he spent at the other halfway houses allowed us to use the knowledge that each had to offer in starting up our operations. The facility is presently set up to handle twelve (12) men.

Residents are asked to agree to spend at least ninety (90) days at this facility before they move on to single family living. They are charged seventy-five ($75.00) a week for room and board. Most of our residents do not have a job when they arrive, no money, and many do not have adequate clothes and toiletries. We help them to find work, and start them on a program of recovery from drug and alcohol abuse. This is done by one-on-one sessions and requiring them to attend a minimum of four plus one in-house meetings of Alcoholics Anonymous a week. They are also required to help with chores at the house.

Our first resident arrived in April, and to date we have served thirty one (31) men. WE currently have ten (10) of these men living at the facility. Twenty one (21) men have been discharged this year. Four (4) of these men left having completed a good program. Six (6) more left, before we thought they were ready to leave, of their own accord. Eleven (11) were asked to leave for breaking house rules or for using alcohol or drugs. We are an equal opportunity house and have had two minority residents to date. One was an African American and one was Hispanic.

The men who were discharged left owing us a total of $1450.00 in back rent that cannot be collected. The money supplied by the four counties is used to cover bad rent debts, insurance, operation expenses, on the facility, and to help defray the salary of the director. We are a not-for-profit organization and are not self-supporting at this point of our operation. We had a net loss of just over $6000.00 for this first year of operations. It is hoped that each county will continue its support at the $3000.00 level for at least one more year. When we have completed the 1996 fiscal year we will have a better idea of what support we will continue to need to have to meet the budget.

Respectfully Yours

William Smith
President Board of Directors

William Kuhn
Director

Summary results from the Indiana Prevention Resource Center's 6th Annual
Alcohol and Other Drug Use Survey

Data collected March and April 1996 in a representative sample of 35 school corporations throughout Indiana. A total of 36.558 students in grades 6 through 12 participated.

The Indiana Prevention Resource Center has coordinated this survey each Spring since 1991. It is funded by a contract with the Indiana Family and Social Services Administration - Division of Mental Health.

SUMMARY OF FINDINGS - 1996

The increased youthful drug use that we reported the last two years continued unabated this year. For the fourth consecutive year, use of marijuana by Indiana children and adolescents has increased -- and is now approaching levels not seen in the past decade. Several years of morale-breaking cutbacks in federal appropriations for school-based drug prevention programs, and the resulting devastation in school-based programming levels and prevention staff layoffs are taking their toll on Hoosier children and adolescents. The significant progress we observed in national statistics from 1980 through 1992 and in Indiana statistics from 1991 through 1992 is now just a memory. Indiana students report increased use of cigarettes, marijuana, inhalants, and most other drugs between 1993 and 1996. Significant findings from the 1996 survey include:

- Monthly use of marijuana by Indiana high school seniors is nearly double the rate reported in 1992 -- increasing from 14.4% in 1992 to 25.2% in 1996. Daily use by seniors jumped from 3.9% in 1992 to 7.6% in 1996! By comparison, a 1995 national survey reported a daily use rate of 4.6% for high school seniors.

- Marijuana use rates among high school sophomores and juniors have now reached nearly the same levels reported by seniors -- erasing the historic trend of grade by grade increases in use rates. This suggests that use is becoming more common at earlier ages and that future increases in the rates reported by seniors may be predicted when these age cohorts reach their senior year.

- Initial experimentation with marijuana is most likely to occur in the 8th and 9th grades, where use rates have more than doubled over the past four years. Nearly twice as many 8th graders as 7th graders reported using marijuana at least once in their lifetimes.

- This trend of increased marijuana use was also reported for 1995 by the National High School Survey (Johnston, et al., 1995), by the PRIDE National Survey, and for Marion County, Indiana by Project I-STAR. Nationally, the upswing in marijuana use in 1993 that reversed a 14-year decline in use from 1978 to 1992, continued in 1995. Positive references to marijuana use continued to increase in popular music, films, and other media.

- Daily, monthly, annual, and lifetime cigarette smoking increased at most grades, which for the third consecutive year, reversing the decline among Hoosier students that we reported in 1992 and 1993. This increase mirrors the increase reported the last three years by the National High School Survey. The increase in cigarette smoking is particularly worrisome, since daily cigarette smoking is the best statistical predictor of future use of alcohol and other drugs (Torabi, Bailey, and Majd-Jabbari, 1993). Among children and adolescents, daily smokers are three times more likely to drink heavily and ten to sixty times more likely to use controlled substances as are non-smokers.

- In 1995, we reported that the one bright spot in the 1995 findings was the decline in rates of binge drinking (consumption of five or more drinks on a single occasion at least once in the two weeks prior to survey). The progress made over the past few years in Indiana appears to have stopped in 1996. Binge drinking rates for 1996 were slightly higher than 1995 for most grade levels, although they still show a significant decline over the past five years. The rates exceed national levels significantly, however.

- On the other hand, use of psychedelic drugs (particularly LSD, but also including mescaline, psilocybin, ecstasy, and others) may be declining somewhat in 1996. It had increased abruptly in 1995. While lifetime and annual use rates continued to increase, monthly use showed a moderate decline in the Spring of 1996. It is too soon to tell if this reflects the start of a long-term decline in use, or is simply an artifact of the cold, damp, late Spring experineced by Indiana in 1996.

- The apparent disproportionately high rate of use of marijuana, cocaine, amphetamines, inhalants, tranquilizers, and narcotics that we reported for the past two years among members of the high school class of 1997 (now 11th graders in 1996) cpontinues to be a concern. The National High School Survey (Johnston, et al., 1994) and the American Alcohol and Drug Survey (Edwards, 1993) both reported increased drug use in this class cohort since 1993. We have observed a dramatic increase in illegal drug use by members of this same class cohort.

- Use of inhalant drugs (nitrous oxide, volatile nitrites, and petroleum-based solvents) also continues to be a problem and appears to be on the increase at most grades and measures of use. Lifetime, annual, and monthly use increased in almost all grades -- many at statistically significant levels. Current (monthly) use is at its greatest level in 8th grade, and annual use is greatest in 9th grade -- both declining in higher grades. Inhalant use is the only observed form of drug use that peaked in the middle grades and then declined. Use of all other drugs increases year-by-year.

- Hoosier students in grades 6 through 12 still maintain their much higher-than-national rates of illegal use of prescription drugs. Use of amphetamines, tranquilizers, and prescription narcotics by Indiana children and adolescents are at rates two to six times higher than reported in the national surveys. The national rates dropped dramatically during the 1980's -- Indiana's present rates are similar to those seen at the national level a decade ago.

- Early experimentation with cigarettes continues to be a problem, with nearly 4% of Hoosier children reporting experimentation with cigarettes by age 7, and more than 9% reporting at least some use by age 9. More than 7% of Hoosier students report at least some use of alcohol prior to age 7 and more than 12% have used alcohol by age 9. This early use of the gateway drugs of tobacco and alcohol may be a major contributor to Indiana's above-the-national average rates of controlled substance use.

- As a matter of fact, nearly all of the increases in other drug use noted in this survey are closely correlated with the increases in cigarette use over the same time frame. If the cigarette smoking rates are artificially adjusted to hold them constant, use of other drugs also remains essentially unchanged. This suggests that nearly all of the increase in other drug use is occurring in the increasingly larger pool of students who choose to smoke cigarettes.

- As reported last year, for all drugs, use by males exceeded use by females. Surprising-

ly, however, there still was significant use of smokeless tobacco and anabolic steroids by female students, despite the fact that these drugs are often assumed by the public to be "male drugs." More than 10% of female juniors and seniors report some use of smokeless tobacco.

ALLEN SUPERIOR COURT

FAMILY RELATIONS DIVISION
715 S. Calhoun Street
Allen County Courthouse, Room 208
Fort Wayne, Indiana 46802-1805
(219) 449-7541

JUDGE ROBERT R. HOCKENSMITH
JUDGE WILLIAM L. BRIGGS
MAGISTRATE CHARLES F. PRATT
MAGISTRATE LORI K. MORGAN

CHIEF JUVENILE PROBATION OFFICER
DOUGLAS R. BROUWER
ASSISTANT CHIEF PROBATION OFFICERS
JULIA A. BRITA
KATHLEEN F. RUSHER
Fax # (219) 449-7432

June 21, 1996

Mark E. Souder
Congressman
U.S. Federal Building
1300 South Harrison Street
Room 3105
Fort Wayne, IN 46802

Dear Congressman Souder,

Allen Superior Court Family Relations Division would like to thank you for giving us the opportunity to share information with regard to our battle against drugs.

In 1987, the Juvenile Court obtained jurisdiction over alcohol offenses once again. Prior to that time, these cases were processed through misdemeanor and traffic court. With the return of alcohol offenses to the juvenile court came the realization that the magnitude of the drug problem in our community warranted a pro-active approach by the juvenile justice system.

In an effort to impact this behavior, Family Relations Division began to develop dispositional alternatives to deal specifically with drug and alcohol related offenses. For the first time, the court began to confiscate the licenses of all young people who appeared in court on alcohol or other drug offenses. Drug and alcohol assessments were being ordered on a regular basis along with counseling and probation supervision.

In 1990, the Family Relations Division began to complete drug testing on all young people detained at Wood Youth Ce
nter regardless of their offense. This testing has proven helpful in assisting juvenile court judges and magistrates in addressing all problems associated with a juvenile's delinquent involvement.

In 1990, the Family Relations Division began to complete drug testing on all young people detained at Wood Youth Center regardless of their offense. This testing has proven helpful in assisting juvenile court Judges and Magistrates in addressing all problems associated with a juvenile's delinquent involvement.

In 1995, there were 3,349 young people tested for drug use when they were admitted to Wood Youth Center. They were tested for THC, cocaine, and alcohol. Forty-four and eight-tenths (44.8) percent of those young people had drugs in their system when they were detained. This percentage does not include those young people picked up on alcohol related offenses which were never sent to the detention center.

The following statistics illustrate the increase in drug referrals over the past ten years.

DRUGS & ALCOHOL	1986	1987	1988	1989	1990	1991	1992	1993	1994	1995
Alcohol Offenses	38	76	179	353	347	373	458	397	349	297
Poss Marijuana	52	49	34	62	49	34	60	63	94	147
Poss. Controlled Sub, incl cocaine	6	5	11	27	41	56	29	19	25	22
Poss. Para.	14	9	19	27	13	5	15	0	23	41
Poss. Lookalike	0	0	0	0	3	0	0	3	0	2
Public Intox.	70	32	24	23	23	29	18	46	26	29
Inhal. Toxic Vapors	0	0	0	5	0	11	5	4	2	3
Visit. Com. Nuis.	7	5	20	39	13	20	17	1	3	0
Dealing Marij.	2	1	3	10	5	4	3	3	6	7
Deal. Cont. Subs. Incl. cocaine	0	0	2	2	2	14	7	10	8	9
Deal. Subs. Rep. as Cont. Subs.	0	0	0	0	7	11	3	0	5	0
Failure to pay Excise Tax	0	0	0	0	0	0	0	0	3	1
	189	177	292	548	509	557	615	546	544	558

Overall increase of 195% (from 189 to 538).
Alcohol offenses increase of 682% (from 38 to 297).
Possession of marijuana increase of 183% (from 52 to 147).
Possession of controlled substance including cocaine increase 267% (from 6 to 22).

The court has developed several specialized programs for young people who have been referred to the court system on drug offenses. These programs have proven to be beneficial.

The court has not been able to continue some of these programs due to the lack of funding. The court would appreciate any consideration for funding of this type of programming.

Respectfully yours,

Robert R. Hockensmith

Robert R. Hockensmith
Judge
Family Relations Division

To: The Honorable Mark Edward Souder
U.S. House of Representatives (IN-4)

From: Kenneth E. Watson
Executive Director
Youth Services Center
Ft. Wayne, Indiana

Date: June 20, 1996

Dear Mr. Souder:

Fort Wayne, Allen County, Indiana, has experienced a dramatic increase in drug-related activity starting in 1985 for both juvenile and adults with the introduction of crack cocaine from the Detroit area. As a result of that increase, the cases filed in the Allen Superior Court, Criminal Division have exploded. In 1988 there were 777 new cases filed. In 1994, 1164 new cases were filed, an increase of approximately 50%. A slightly larger amount (1173) was filed in 1993. The felony filing rate for 1995 shows an approximate 12% increase over 1994. Estimates from the law enforcement agencies in Allen County place the percentage of those cases being drug-related at 75-80%. In 1994, Allen County experienced a record number of homicides, 41, in a community of approximately 300,000. The Chief of Police of Fort Wayne has indicated that approximately 45% of those homicides were related to gang activity. Fort Wayne has also experienced a great increase in the number of gangs. The principal activity of those gangs is dealing in drugs. A large amount of the gang leaders come from Detroit, Michigan.

In 1990, after a survey involving urinalysis testing of all persons brought into the Allen County Jail showed that 75% of all persons tested, tested positive for some drug. The Allen Superior Court, Criminal Division, in an attempt to help stem the tide of drug dealing in Allen County instituted a policy relating to drug dealing offenses: All persons charged with drug dealing offenses had their bonds increased from the normal bond of $10,000 to $50,000. To deal with the jail crowding situation that such an increase caused, drug dealing cases were placed on an expedited trial docket, with the goal of bringing those type of cases to trial within 70 days. Additionally, the court took the position of requiring a minimum executed prison sentence of 3 years. The Court hoped that such a policy would have the effect of decreasing the number of drug sales in the community. Unfortunately, this policy did not have the desired effect. There was no significant decrease in this type of case.

Several years ago, the Fort Wayne Chief of Police instituted a policy of targeting the drug users, in an attempt to decrease the amount of drug-related activity in Fort Wayne. The thought was that if users were taken off the streets, the demand for drugs would decrease, therefore reducing the amount of drug dealing, that policy also did not have the desired effect, and was abandoned.

Due to the increased caseload experienced by the Allen Superior Court, Criminal Division, the three judges of that division determined that it was necessary to hire a magistrate to help with the judicial overload. Once the approval of the County Council was obtained for the hiring of an additional magistrate, the judges decided that it was desirable to institute a Drug Court to implement the innovative procedures that other Courts have utilized to deal with the ever-increasing drug problem in the United States. The judges assigned the Honorable Kenneth R. Scheibenberger to the yet to be formed Drug Court for Allen County and gave him the task of formulating the policies and procedures for that new court. Since January 1, 1995, Judge Scheibenberger has been hearing only drug possession and drug dealing cases, in addition to doing many hours of research and community contacts regarding the implementation of the new Drug Court. He has determined that it is impossible to begin the Drug Court without additional funding sources, since Allen County, like almost all local jurisdictions, has no additional funds available for implementation of this program.

In 1994, 270 felony drug cases were filed in the Allen Superior Court, Criminal Division. Felony drug cases include only those cases involving possession of drugs or paraphernalia as well as those cases in which dealing in drugs is charged. For 1995, the rate of filing is similar, giving the court no reason to believe that those cases will decrease. The Court is still using the expedited disposition of dealing cases detailed above, while the possession cases are being dealt with in the same manner as all other felony cases. While dealing cases are being handled in a very short time frame, the possession cases typically are set for trial within 150 days of arrest and initial hearing, however, there are many instances of trials being continued at both the request of the State as well as the defendant, resulting in lengthier disposition times. Incarceration is principally relied on as the disposition method for the dealing cases, while probation is the typical disposition for the first time drug possessor. The terms of probation in every instance include the requirement that the offender receive substance abuse counseling monitored by the Probation Officer. Other requirements almost always include obtaining a GED, high school diploma or vocational training, as well as some form of community service. Often times a condition of probation includes Home Detention.

As in most jurisdictions, the Probation Department is overloaded due to the great increase in felony filings. In Allen County the typical caseload of a Probation officer is 200 offenders. Obviously, supervision of all these offenders is next to impossible. The Probation Department has recently instituted a "zero-tolerance" policy, which has had the effect of greatly increasing this Court's caseload of probation violators. Approximately 50% of those violators are returning to court because they tested positive for drugs when a random urinalysis was taken.

When one looks at the material, certain facts emerge. 1) Higher volume in the criminal courts. 2) 75% of all arrests have some type of substance in their system upon apprehension. 3) 50% of offenders regardless of disposition of sentencing (jail or social programs) return to the system for drug usage. 4) More police officers are being hired which in turn increases the arrest rate with other parts of the system such as Public Defenders and Prosecutors, Hearing Officers, and Probation Officers are lacking in resources and personnel for the ever increasing degree of drug-related offenses. Because of treatment philosophy that was developed in the 1960's up to today, we have developed a treatment "merry-go-round" where offenders bounce from one treatment program to another. There is a concern that we have lost accountability in the Criminal Justice System because of this philosophy. The central issue is how do we hold offenders accountable while offering treatment for substance abuse problems. The first step is good assessment of the offender when they enter the system. There are individuals who like drugs and the drug life style. They use the concept of treatment as a ploy or con to avoid consequences. Treatment dollars are wasted on this group and raises a certain question, how many times can you be enrolled in a treatment program or is relapse just a permanent state of the treatment "merry-go-round".

Let me address juvenile issues. There is no question crack cocaine enters into the development of gangs and violence on the street. However, in our area the three drugs of choice are tobacco, alcohol, and marijuana. Older adolescents 15 and 16 years old have a higher usage especially if they were arrested for a drug related offense. As you are well aware the drug usage of adolescents has a tremendous impact on teenage pregnancies, school drop outs, and single parent families. Here again the system is lacking in good assessments for adolescents at the front end of the system.

Concerning drug usage and the life style associated with it. I find a lot of money spent on talk that is ineffective with an action oriented population. We have been able to collect a lot of data that is somewhat lacking in performance base evaluation. With all that is said and done, it is my opinion that systems need to design approaches and strategies to carry out their functions. There is roll confusion within the Criminal Justice System. The system should act as a stop sign with its major goal of protecting the public and leave treatment up to the mental health and treatment community or correction personnel. These are just some thoughts for your field hearing that will be held in Fort Wayne on June 24th.

○

9780160557392

S. Hrg. 107–1032

FUTURE OF INSURING TERRORISM RISKS

HEARING

BEFORE THE

COMMITTEE ON COMMERCE, SCIENCE, AND TRANSPORTATION UNITED STATES SENATE

ONE HUNDRED SEVENTH CONGRESS

FIRST SESSION

OCTOBER 30, 2001

Printed for the use of the Committee on Commerce, Science, and Transportation

U.S. GOVERNMENT PRINTING OFFICE

91–957 PDF WASHINGTON : 2004

For sale by the Superintendent of Documents, U.S. Government Printing Office
Internet: bookstore.gpo.gov Phone: toll free (866) 512–1800; DC area (202) 512–1800
Fax: (202) 512–2250 Mail: Stop SSOP, Washington, DC 20402–0001

SENATE COMMITTEE ON COMMERCE, SCIENCE, AND TRANSPORTATION

ONE HUNDRED SEVENTH CONGRESS

FIRST SESSION

ERNEST F. HOLLINGS, South Carolina, *Chairman*

DANIEL K. INOUYE, Hawaii	JOHN McCAIN, Arizona
JOHN D. ROCKEFELLER IV, West Virginia	TED STEVENS, Alaska
JOHN F. KERRY, Massachusetts	CONRAD BURNS, Montana
JOHN B. BREAUX, Louisiana	TRENT LOTT, Mississippi
BYRON L. DORGAN, North Dakota	KAY BAILEY HUTCHISON, Texas
RON WYDEN, Oregon	OLYMPIA J. SNOWE, Maine
MAX CLELAND, Georgia	SAM BROWNBACK, Kansas
BARBARA BOXER, California	GORDON SMITH, Oregon
JOHN EDWARDS, North Carolina	PETER G. FITZGERALD, Illinois
JEAN CARNAHAN, Missouri	JOHN ENSIGN, Nevada
BILL NELSON, Florida	GEORGE ALLEN, Virginia

KEVIN D. KAYES, *Democratic Staff Director*
MOSES BOYD, *Democratic Chief Counsel*
MARK BUSE, *Republican Staff Director*
JEANNE BUMPUS, *Republican General Counsel*